HERE'S
TO 30+
YEARS!

Enjoy

Ned

RETIRED!

What do you want to do for the next 30 years?

Ted Buckley

First Edition Design Publishing
Sarasota, Florida USA

Retired! What do you want to do for the next 30 years?
Copyright ©2022 Ted Buckley

ISBN 978-1506-907-27-7 HCJ
ISBN 978-1506-907-26-0 PBK
ISBN 978-1506-907-28-4 EBK

LCCN 2022901103

January 2022

Published and Distributed by
First Edition Design Publishing, Inc.
P.O. Box 17646, Sarasota, FL 34276-3217
www.firsteditiondesignpublishing.com

Although the author and publisher have made every effort to ensure that the information in this book was correct at press time, the author and publisher do not assume and hereby disclaim any liability to any party for any loss, damage, or disruption caused by errors or omissions, whether such errors or omissions result from negligence, accident, or any other cause.

Securities offered through Triad Advisors, LLC. Member FINRA/SIPC. Advisory Services offered through Triad Hybrid Solutions LLC, a registered investment advisor. Mooney Lyons Financial Advisors and Triad Advisors, LLC are not affiliated. Investing in securities involves risk of loss that clients should be prepared to bear. No investment process is free of risk; no strategy or risk management technique can guarantee returns or eliminate risk in any market environment. There is no guarantee that your investment will be profitable. **Past performance is not a guide to future performance.** The value of investments, as well any investment income, is not guaranteed and can fluctuate based on market conditions.

Mooney Lyons Advisors does not offer legal or tax advice. Please consult the appropriate professional regarding your individual circumstance.

I'm dedicating this book to all my clients and everyone getting ready or in the retirement phase of their lives

Reading this book is designed to be an active experience for you to get the most out of it. Please download the Free Companion workbook at www.TedBuckley.com. Additional worksheets and updates are included.

Acknowledgements

I understand that no one gets to where they are in life without the help and guidance of many people. I am thanking my wife, Kelly McGrath Buckley, as the love of my life and my foundational rock. After meeting at St. Norbert college, we've been through it all! My four adult children, Joe, Jack, Sam, and Ali, who, as a parent, I feel I learn as much from them as hopefully, they learn from me. I had two loving and inspirational parents, Art and Kay, and my brothers, Glen and Bob, and my sister, Con. Kelly also opened her side of the family to more relationships and love, especially from her mom and dad!

I learn and grow from all my relationships along the way from friends at Meadowbrook Grade School, Glenbrook North High School in Northbrook, St. Norbert College, where I was a member of their hockey team, and Phi Sigma Epsilon Fraternity in De Pere, WI, to the Sleepy Hollow area, Toastmasters, Dental Trade Alliance, Multi-Sport Madness Triathlon Club, Barrington Bike Club, and Boulder Ridge Golf Country Club.

My old bosses, teachers, and coaches helped me develop in countless ways, along with my learning experiences and friendships formed with co-workers at Interpore, Lifecore Biomedical, and Bisco Dental.

Thank you to everyone who volunteers to give back because of a calling or an inspiration to help others – Volunteer Coaches, Volunteers at Boys and Girls Clubs, Chicago Dental Society Foundation, Knights of Columbus, Sleepy Hollow Service Club. Thank you to my spiritual inspiration at St. Catherine of Siena in West Dundee, especially all my fellow parishioners and leaders, including Fr. John McNamara, Fr. Matthew Deblock, and Deacon Hank Schmalen.

I also want to especially thank my team that surrounds me every day at Mooney Lyons Financial Advisors. This includes Keith Mooney, Joe Lyons, Greg Scheider, Nadine Scheider, Jason Randl, Jeff Scheider, Shawna Scheider, Lucas Wandell, Bret Mooney, Eric Mesko, Misty Parrillo, and Cindy Jacobs. We work hard, have fun, and never forget to put the needs of our clients first—we never forget that is why we do what we do!

My clients inspire me every day with a reminder of the tremendous amount of responsibility we have! They are hardworking people to get to where they are, and each with their own personalities looking towards me and Mooney Lyons to put them in the best possible position to meet their goals and reach their dreams.

In writing this book, I was able to get input from a variety of friends and work associates. Brian Geddes was a true help in shaping the writing of this book. The team at Stellar Edge Marketing Group in West Dundee helped develop the look and feel of the creative side of the book.

Thank you to all listed, and I apologize if I forgot to mention anyone!

About Ted's Financial Consulting Practice

Ted understands that life can be overwhelming, busy, and hectic. That is why he works with his clients as a fiduciary financial advisor, who many of his clients call the CFO of their family. As Chief Financial Officer of your household, Ted will prepare and update a financial game plan that is in line with your goals and financial wellbeing.

As a group, Mooney Lyons manages over half a billion dollars of assets. Ted works with select client families where he feels he can have the greatest impact, so he has time to focus on each situation personally. Ted is your direct advocate, leveraging the 13 team members in his office to uncomplicate your financial goals.

Any successful plan has more than one part. Ted and his team monitor your investments and financial plan and adjust along the way and coordinate the efforts of your attorney and CPA to ensure all parts are aligned.

Ted is very active in the local community and focuses his efforts on those groups to assist those in need. Ted is on the Chicago Dental Society Foundation board and the Boys and Girls Club of Dundee Township and is also an active member of St. Catherine's Knights of Columbus and Sleepy Hollow Service Club.

Ted graduated from St. Norbert College in De Pere, Wisconsin, with a Bachelor of Business Administration. Ted is married to his college sweetheart, Kelly, and together they have four young adult children. He enjoys golf, playing acoustic guitar, and volunteer work. He is also an avid Chicago sports fan.

Education:

CERTIFIED PLAN FIDUCIARY ADVISOR (CPFA)

Series 7 registration – General Securities Representative

Series 66 registration – Uniform Combined State Law

Illinois health and life insurance producer licenses

tedb@mooneylyons.com

847-382-2600 office

Introduction

Soon, God willing, the morning will come when you wake and perform your workday routine for the final time. You'll wake up, take a shower, and do all your typical morning routines. You'll drive to work like normal, but something will be different. You'll feel it, and you'll know it because it's your last day of work. It may be your choice; it may be your employer's. Either way, the decision has been made, and your retirement is today. At the end of your last day, you'll say your goodbyes and make your final rush hour commute. As you walk through the front door, carrying a box of your office stuff, you'll announce, "Honey, I'm home from my last day at work! What do you want to do for the next 30 years?"

Maybe you've already retired and still haven't decided what to do with those 30 years. Well, it's never too late to adjust your frame of mind. After all:

The *FUTURE* is yours.
You've been paying for it.
How are you going to use it?

That's my question. How are you going to use your future? That's it. That's the whole point of my book. If you already know how you will use your future, you're ahead of the game and have saved yourself the time it'll take to read this book. Put it down and get back to that streaming series about the people from another reality with the blue glowy thing that destroys planets.

Your future is ready.

If that's not the case, I can help.

I want you to understand my purpose for this book.

This book DOES NOT focus on:

- Income Distribution
- Expense Planning
- Diversification
- Tax Planning
- Legacy Trusts
- Charitable Giving
- Social Security Strategies

I work on all the above, every day, for my clients. What's come to amaze me as a financial advisor is that we spend most of our retirement planning energy on building the financial foundation and developing a retirement plan. The retirement plan we run is very important to evaluate income distribution, tax efficiency, and develop legacy planning ideas. We do not typically cover *"The WHAT and the WHY"* in detail— those things that will make you happy in retirement. But that's ok. I got you covered. *The What and the Why* are the purposes of this book. This book is for the period after *all* the work is done, the actual 'next' after your career life when you activate a financially realized retirement. You need to discover those things that make you happy, and it's not easy. It takes time, and *The WHAT and the WHY* may change over time.

I looked for books to recommend to near retiring or retired clients and never found what I thought offered enough helpful information. Instead of recommending sub-par books, I decided there was a huge need to write a guidebook to help people get ready and enjoy retirement to the fullest and have the time of their lives.

What do you need to do to have the time of your life for the next 30 years? What's going to make you happy? I'll tell you right now. It's simple—just one thing. You have to answer a question. That question is: "Who Are You?"

It's an age-old question and a Who song, where Roger Daltrey sings the refrain 158 times, including stutters.

Other than water, fiber, and bones, the 'you' inside is that small part of your brain over which you exercise free will or at least a good imitation of it. That's the part that can influence emotion, in that you can make choices that you have a pretty good idea will make you happy.

And you should be pretty good at it. Thus far, you have made life choices that got you to a retirement where you have options.

The current you is not who was there 25 years ago when you thought bidding on a Michael Jordan basketball at a school auction was so vital that you spent an embarrassing amount of money to win it. Now maybe you have other priorities. Perhaps they are simple, like eating healthier, or perhaps your focus is bidding on a collectible Corvette that makes the basketball price seem like pocket change.

Financial Preparation **+** **Mental Preparation** **=** Happy Retirement

A companion workbook can be printed at tedbuckley.com to help you ***Mentally Prepare for A Happy Retirement***. My hope is that the exercises in the workbook:

1. Will challenge you and your partner–not all the answers are easy, but you will learn something about yourself and each other.
2. Will be used over and over every year or so. Your answers will change as your retirement evolves.
3. Will take away some of the fear and unknowns about retirement—you worked hard, saved money, many times put your children or your parents first, and now it's YOUR turn to enjoy your life! It's time to plan and prioritize this next life stage.

That's fortunate because what I've found as a financial advisor is that many people do a fine job of 'paying the bill' of retirement but don't spend much time thinking about the purpose of their retirement.

Too many people simply pay the bill as if retirement is a utility. I'd say that's an excellent way to build a habit of saving for retirement, but it may not be the best way of actually putting that retirement to a fun and fulfilling use.

Gas is easy to use once the pilot is lit. Electricity is easy to use once you know how to operate a light switch. But no matter how well-lit the countertops or how great the kitchen range is, making a good meal is something else.

And you pretty much have to come up with your own personal recipe for retirement.

With life expectancy being what it is today (78.5 years), healthy people can expect to enjoy around two decades of shiny happy retirement. Many people are enjoying a healthy retirement into their 80's or 90's. That's the good news. Unfortunately, many people have unexpected health issues that can derail all the fun plans. You must prepare for stages of retirement that will hit all of us one way or another.

Remember graduating? Getting married? The birth of your first child? The first solid career move that you knew would pay for it all. Retirement is that feeling of hitting a milestone, again, and the first thing you realize is that this one is quite different—it's a big milestone, and you need to be ready mentally. During retirement, you will face some very challenging times, such as declining health, the death of a spouse, or other adverse events.

But you will also have the potential to live 20 to 30 years with a life of fulfillment and happiness that you never thought possible. I hope to give you new ideas, inspire some of your own, and perhaps help define how to progress with ideas you already have. I want you to learn more about yourself, your relationships with others, and how you can use that understanding to build activities that will drive your soul.

You have control over your day-to-day mental outlook, so although we cannot know our long-term health prognosis, we can live with a lifestyle that can increase our odds of success. One of the most important points I can communicate to a client is that you can expect health to fluctuate over your retirement, but you should still plan for the overall duration of your retirement to be two to three decades.

When you start thinking about retirement, some thoughts about your impending transition will likely go through your head. However, no two retirement experiences are the same, and each transition in life involves a combination of fear, excitement, and confusion. Multidimensional preparation for retirement is essential. No two people experience retirement the same way. This goes for husbands *and* wives. It's a process. It doesn't happen all at once. It takes time.

Long before you get to the point of creating the day-to-day shape of your retirement, you need to give some thought as to what that shape will look like. It's a lot easier to draw a circle than turn a square into a circle. That's why a good financial advisor can be essential in laying out the foundation.

It's the financial advisor's job to help you clarify your retirement savings goals and develop a realistic way to achieve them. A good financial advisor sets you up, so your retirement is a time when you get to live as many dreams as your health and finances will support. While bucket lists will change over time, I love when clients get in the habit of communicating what they want retirement to look like.

- Imagine what kind of life you want to lead after you stop working.
- Outline these goals, so your advisor knows what to plan.
- Stick with the plan.
- Adjust as needed.

There are thousands of factors that can affect your ability to maintain your financial confidence regarding retirement planning. With the help of an advisor who appreciates the goal and methods used to build wealth, you can live out the retirement you want. First, you have to know what that looks like.

So, let's get started!!

Chapter One

Realistic Expectations

You've likely sent a kid or two to college. If so, you've certainly discussed how college is a perfect place to invent or reinvent oneself. Retirement is the same type of thing! NOW is the time to reinvent yourself, live your dreams—don't settle for ho-hum—be bold—be the best you!

You have just entered a brand-new stage in your life and are about to face massive lifestyle changes and opportunities. Don't just slouch toward retirement because this is the last stage of your life, and you think you're done. The curtain is opening on your closing act, and it's going to be an epic performance. Plus, you may not get an encore. It should feel great to know you have potentially one-third of your life in front of you full of significance and excitement. It is time to develop a thoughtful, balanced plan of what a happy retirement looks like to you.

Keep in mind that age imposes limitations, and going skydiving is probably not a reasonable expectation for everybody. But don't sell yourself short on your dreams. The reason why people say that age is just a number is because it is. The good news is that a purposeful life in retirement is possible, and many seniors find it. Have realistic expectations and build this part of your life by planning exciting and meaningful experiences with family, and friends, blending hobbies and social activities to create a well-rounded life.

As an adult, you've identified with your profession, family, friends, and family members. But when you settle into retirement, sometimes you find it hard to create a new identity when your focus shifts.

It may take time and even more effort to achieve a version of you ready to participate in a fulfilling retirement, but it is worth it. After all, you did not get to where you are today by avoiding life's challenges. Like adjusting to college or your first job with serious responsibilities and tangible compensations, you had to adapt your style, manner, and lifestyle to fit the new situation. It's the same with retirement. Only this time the boss is you! You set the rules. If you want to give yourself a boatload of vacation days, that is up to you. While you are at it, give yourself a raise. You deserve it!

As with any significant change in life, you will feel more comfortable embracing this new phase of life once you have firm ground under your feet. Keep in mind that this ground doesn't have to be your home ground. You can do things that a work-life didn't allow easily, like traveling the world with your partner and living abroad while writing the book you've always wanted to write.

I see retirement as having five stages. They don't necessarily go in any particular order. One stage may happen twice or more. For example, you may deal with an illness from which you recover. Your energy may wane, but then you do something like make a drastic diet change, learn meditation, find good supplements, and you feel your full capacities coming back. So, here's an overview of the five stages, and then I'll go into more detail about each:

5 Stages of Retirement

1. **Honeymoon** - Finally! But you don't yet have a working understanding that it's not a two-week summer camp full of fun and excitement.

2. **Settling In** – You've got a great routine. You're enjoying life. You're healthy and on a roll.

3. **You've Got This** - Now professionally retired, you know the places to buy gas for less, the good restaurants and what they have for specials, and where to travel off-season.

4. **Slowing Down** - You can't ride that bike so much anymore, but a walk is good too, no more lifting the grandchildren. Climbing the Grand Canyon is out.

5. **Health Limitations** - You saw this happen to others; You just did not think it would happen to you— Cancer, Chronic Pain, Injuries, Alzheimer's, etc.

"How long does each stage last?"

That's the question I'm asked most frequently. Of course, it varies greatly, but the average is somewhere between 3 to 9 years per stage.

A lot depends on the age at which you retire. A particular stage may last ten years for you—that's fine. The reason I break retirement into stages is so you're aware and make the most of what you can accomplish as you pass through each stage.

Honeymoon Stage

The overriding key to facilitating the transition to this phase is planning and preparation. You have accomplished awesome things throughout your life. Retirement can bring you that same feeling of achievement and satisfaction. You got where you are now by planning, focusing on your strengths, and keeping your eye on the ball. Continue in that vein, and you will transition to the settling-in stage of your retirement like a pro.

It's a unique and freeing experience to witness the vanishing of your old organizational routine, reaction to pressures, tolerance of the millions of feelings you have each week from associates and higher-ups.

But, then poof, it's gone. Everything suddenly feels so much lighter, and you are free to shift your attention and focus to what is vital as you progress through this phase of your life.

Remember those dreams where you went to work naked? A psychologist might tell you that such a dream means you feel unprepared about something. Many clients have told me that they wake up in the morning the first few weeks of retirement thinking they are running late for a meeting at work—then smile, rollover, and remember, there's isn't anything they have to prepare for unless they want to prepare for it.

Many times, one partner may retire before the other. In consideration of the working partner, the early retired partner may make sure they don't sleep in. They may even have coffee and yogurt ready for the working spouse and prepare everything they need for the day. Then after the working spouse leaves, you can lay on the couch and get some extra sleep. I'm kidding here. Get your act together and get ready for your new day!

If you want to build a new purpose in life, you must find activities that fulfill your new identity. You want the ability to make sure you have the finances to achieve what you want. And you want to spend your time doing what you want to do, not what your employer, boss, or even your family members and spouse want. Retirement is fun and rewarding when it is thoughtfully planned and well-executed.

I recommend planning a couple of big activities to kick off your retirement. About six months before retiring, begin a plan for something you haven't been able to do because of work constraints. Spread out a couple of big activities for the first year to 18 months. Just having these set up will give you fun things to look forward to on the horizon. Then, when friends and coworkers ask, "So what do you plan to do for retirement," you'll have an answer.

If you keep hearing yourself say, "I don't know," you may start feeling unsure of yourself. When coming up on retirement, you *need* something to look forward to.

I have clients, Tom and Tina, and during the first year of their retirement, they went on four extended trips. While they spent more than they had planned, they said it was worth it because it got the long-deprived desire to travel out of their system. Tom's career was such that he had no free time to travel—so for him, that was super important. Now that they have been retired for six years, they still enjoy traveling but don't feel a *need* to travel.

Perhaps the best way to plan for retirement is to imagine the future and focus on where you will spend it. The possibility to imagine today what your needs and wishes might be in the future is perhaps the most critical aspect of your planning. Ask yourself what will your future look like and what will be your wishes, needs, and goals for your retirement?

Every day is new, and they all belong entirely to you—until they don't. So, as you move through this phase, keep in mind to find joy each day and understand that this too shall pass!

Settling In Stage

You're finding your footing—learning about new things you like and what you don't.

You are developing a great routine.

You're enjoying life.

You and your partner are healthy and continuing to learn what you love about each other.

You feel good, and life IS good!

You are past the Honeymoon stage when everything is new and exciting. You have had time to unwind career stress and develop your retirement mode. At this stage, the dream of doing what you want—enjoying activities and decelerating life's pace becomes relaxing, doable, and enjoyable. You have joined groups and tried things that went well. Some you want to continue to make a part of your routine and some you don't want to pursue—maybe you like pickleball or you don't—either way, the Settling In stage gives you a chance to find your groove at your pace and see what's out there.

Settling In does not mean you have perfected retirement, and neither does it mean you're stuck in a routine forever. Your passion and the groups you like will change over the course of retirement. For example, my wife is a member of a local volunteer group and met a new member—let's say her name is Jenny Joiner. After they exchanged pleasantries, my wife asked Jenny what brought her to the group. Jenny noted the other organization she had been a member in for seven years had new people running it and had changed their focus from helping the local community to being more committed to world concerns. Jenny wanted to keep her focus local.

My point is not to say which is a better group to join, but Jenny gets a gold star in her attitude of not letting the changing group get you down. She found a new commitment that was a better fit and started over. Unhappy retired people are the ones who say, yeah, "I tried that once ten years ago, and it was not fun." Really? Wouldn't you tell your 8-year-old granddaughter that if she did not like the flute lessons, maybe she would like piano or maybe soccer? Be curious and open to new things—you only have one go at this life, and YOU can make it remarkable.

One way many retirees find fulfillment in retirement is to volunteer their time and work. Although this can be challenging, rebalancing occurs as retirees move quickly through this next phase of retirement, feel a loss of redundant goals, and start assessing their experiences. The idea of service, becoming part of a force for good, can be gratifying and life-affirming.

You've Got This Stage

Once you have built up a new retirement identity, you can enjoy your retirement as it should be. For many retirees, it is enough to live in freedom, try new things, enjoy a life of endless possibilities and be content with a simpler life. It is essential to find something that brings meaning in any stage of life but finding meaning becomes crucial in retirement. Activities such as pursuing your passions or adding new fun activities to your daily life are great ways to avoid loneliness and falling into the blues.

If you find this book helpful, perhaps you will have gained some confidence in your first few years of retirement in trying new things and understanding it's okay to not have had all optimal experiences.

You may find a new group to join and leave when you find out you're not jelling with them. Also, maybe you have some new friends in the neighborhood or the clubs you like, such as playing cards or the morning walk group.

The point of the "YOU GOT THIS" section is to realize you're like the senior in college who can give the freshman advice and be admired by them as someone who has their act together and is walking with a figurative strut.

King of The Hill may be an overstatement, but you're through early retirement and have some experiences under your belt by now. You can share what you learned in your first stages of retirement—how you learned to adjust and change.

Don't give up trying new stuff, and when you catch yourself saying, "Oh, I did something like before, and it was not fun," do five burpees for punishment.

My wife and I recently bought a condo near Lake Geneva, Wisconsin, and at the town's big summer event, I sent a text to a good friend who we don't see very often. He has a house in the neighborhood just a few miles up the road from our condo. We asked them to come down and hang out. We had a picnic table with two extra spots reserved for them.

When they joined us, the stories and laughs were non-stop. It was fun to share that time with friends. My buddy was facing the lake and looking at the sunset when he commented, "This lake is so beautiful, and I have not seen it all summer." My wife and I looked startled and could not imagine living five minutes from the lake and not visiting it often. Still, our friends had been busy working on their house and not taking time out to enjoy the reason they owned in the area.

Remember, don't fall into a rut—don't take things for granted—look up, look around, and take it all in!

Slowing Down Stage

At some point in retirement, you might look around and wonder if you made a mistake. Retirement is getting repetitious. You've lost a feeling of relevance you had when you were working. You're starting to think that retirement isn't as fun as you had expected.

I think that every time a person, myself included, contemplates retirement, even if it's for 15 minutes on a sunny Saturday morning, while you're having your coffee and scrolling through your phone, an idea strolls into view. The idea that we are planning for the day when walking the dog is no longer an early morning pleasure. Soon after, it becomes a knee-biting chore, and then it becomes one more thing that will no longer be possible.

At first, it's common to look forward to "slowing down" or "relaxing" at this stage in life. However, 'slowing down' seems oppressive when it's a forced decline caused by entropy more than anything else.

Slowing down can grant you some creativity to focus on enjoyable activities that may be less physically challenging. For example, instead of hiking in the woods, maybe a pleasant stroll around the neighborhood is more in order. Fit the things you like into something that you can physically and mentally enjoy. Perhaps night driving is hard now, so either take an Uber at night or keep to daytime activities.

Golf is an excellent example of an activity you can modify. You can go from playing 18 holes to playing nine holes. Playing from a shorter tee box makes the game fun when you are not hitting the ball as far.

Ok—here is a pep talk: You are no longer 30 years old, so what is the point of a (now fading) testosterone and endorphin rush that comes from showing off for others? You are finding deeper enjoyment for yourself. So put the ego aside. It's dangerous. It can make you lonely and sad, wishing for your younger days. You may not be able to do a 5k run, but you can do a one-mile fun walk. Or even volunteer for running events—these events always need helpers!

Health Limitations Stage

Chronic diseases are no fun, and health declines are the thing that scares people the most when thinking about aging from any angle, retirement or otherwise. Some health problems can include high blood pressure, high cholesterol, obesity, diabetes, heart disease, and cancer. Whether you skate through retirement without significant illness or injury or end up plagued by constant health issues, it's essential to plan and be prepared to deal with whatever comes down the pipeline.

It is difficult to know precisely how many people live with chronic diseases. For example, the Alzheimer's Association reports that about 11 percent of adults in the United States, or about 2.5 million people, have Alzheimer's, or about 1.2 million Americans. According to the CDC, this accounts for about one-third of all cognitive impairment cases in adults over 65. Experts concede that more than two-thirds of those with cognitive impairments will live for at least another ten years after diagnosis.

The National Osteoporosis Foundation estimates that 54 million Americans over the age of 50 are affected by low bone mass or osteoporosis, putting them at high risk of fractures and osteoarthritis. This condition can cause bone loss, arthritis, and other health problems.

Diabetes, coronary heart disease, and cancer are common in the elderly. However, according to the US Centers for Disease Control and Prevention, cardiovascular disease is the leading cause of death in Americans aged 65 and older. In addition, metabolic syndrome, which affects 50% of people over 60, can cause long-term health problems such as diabetes and cardiovascular disease.

Plan for Some Peaks and Valleys

Throughout your retirement, you'll have physical challenges. It's not necessarily a gradual or a steep decline. Though it can be either of those. Most often it's an up and down. You might go through a bout with cancer. If you've been lucky enough to find it early, you can feel better than ever in a few years, and be back on top of all your plans.

Preparation is key, both mentally and financially. Stay aware and enjoy each stage while you are in it. No stage lasts forever, and if you are on the injured reserve list and can't play your desired sport or activity right now, spend the time in physical therapy and build up your body while experiencing other activities to fill the void.

Questions

1. What stage of retirement are you in?

2. What do you know about your current stage, and what can you expect?

Chapter Two

Know Yourself and Your Partner

Personality, Behavior, and Values

Learn About Yourself

You may be surprised to learn what makes you tick! I'm not asking you to go on a long, arduous journey of self-discovery. The Fellini films or documentaries you rented in the 1980s cover that kind of self-discovery (and you didn't even have to watch them, just renting them earns you existential points, double if you didn't return the movies).

I'm asking that you be ready to challenge yourself and have a good time with it—be all in!

Please don't get stuck into what I call destructive circular beliefs. Just because something is true today doesn't make it accurate forever and ever.

This kind of thinking can limit you and your happiness. You can say, "I don't like sushi," even though you never tried it. But why? Or "I don't enjoy going to the beach because 30 years ago, a seagull pooped on my head." I hoped you smiled at that. If you made a list of all the things you don't like and then tried them again, do you think the list would remain static? Probably not. Some things would come off, with, likely, a few additions.

Think about each decade of your life. You evolve slowly, first the recent grad, then a new career person, marriage and kids may come next, and you still have to prove that you can achieve, so after you get used to kids, you become the overachiever at work. You're in shape and out of shape. You party too much, party just right, then you're too old to do much of that anymore. You lose old friends and gain new ones. Your life has been an evolution waiting for some input from *you*.

In many ways, before retirement, daily schedules were forced upon us. We had to *squeeze* in our free time fun. Many of us have also had very stressful jobs where we had to play the game to be successful. After many years, it was hard to draw the line between the work persona and the person at home. At work, you may have been a hard-driving manager pushing for more sales, while the at-home, you were easy-going and just wanted to be mellow. But then something happened. Over time the line between the two *of you* began to merge. You may have become snappy, crabby, and demanding of your spouse and children.

But now that you're retiring, you no longer have to gloss over your true self. It's nice and liberating at times to be free!!!

Those are some reasons why people who used to be overly stressed and tense—road rage kind of people—are now taking the time to smell the roses and appreciate all the good they have around them after retirement. As a result, these folks tend to feel they are living a more meaningful life.

Self-evaluation can be scary. We don't want to admit the stuff we don't like about ourselves, and that's primarily for two reasons. First, we don't want to uncover things about ourselves that may define us as a true and irrevocable jerk. The second reason is that we like to believe we are truly unique. Of course, we're all a bit unique, but it's like the kids who want to have long hair to be unique – just like all the other kids with long hair in their friend group. What's important is that it's *NOW* that you can freely explore uniqueness.

My point is do not be afraid of yourself and the things you now get to explore. Change is not always necessary unless you feel that it's vital to your self-understanding.

This is important – Please do yourself a favor and set aside an evening or a rainy afternoon that you can put on Ed Sheeran, Chicago, Beatles, or your favorite Spotify channel – relax and enjoy the following exercises. Relax and dive in. Whether you're single, newly married, married 35 years or living with your partner, this self-discovery is the first step.

> **Step 1** – Read the complete chapter first. Then it is time to complete the exercises, separately from your partner. Take your time – maybe an hour discovering and using the workbook independently.
>
> **Step 2** – Have your partner guess your results.
>
> **Step 3** – Share your information with your partner. Discuss and share with your partner your scores and your self-observations.

This conversation should be fun and possibly a bit surprising—be patient and be understanding.

Later in the book, we'll talk about bucket lists. I look at the above steps as a preliminary step to discovering content for a future bucket list of activities and goals you can do together and areas that you will either do independently or with family and friends.

We all change, and this chapter has two parts to answer the question, "Who are you?"

- Your **Personality and Behavior** - What are your dominant characteristics.

- What are your **Core Values** - What is most important to you?

There are really three common ways to uncover the data we need to determine these things:

1. See a counselor or therapist for a few weeks or years, and they can get a clear picture of who THEY think you are.

2. Subscribe to a variety of courses or online tests that will charge you to uncover some ideas of who you are.

3. Complete the work in this chapter, which will guide you through a journey of self-discovery and who is at your core – Personality, Behavior, and Values!

I have read extensively on these subjects, attended many sessions on life coaching, and completed many corporate personality motivation and leadership development courses. However, I am not a trained therapist, and the exercises in this book are not intended as medical advice. If you have a serious or ongoing condition that you are currently seeking medical attention or feel you need additional care, you should follow the advice of your physician.

Many people have been given Myers-Briggs, DISC personality or various other behavior tests during their working careers. Or they've been to a therapist or a psychologist to learn about themselves. That's great. Employers, many times will give a test to potential or existing employees to learn more about what makes them tick. These are accepted in some circles and other circles do not prescribe to those philosophies. Look at this section as guiding you through a rough draft of uncovering aspects of yourself you may not be aware of. Each time you complete it; you refine your self-knowledge.

The reason I included this section in the book was to include a customized two-part self-evaluation geared specifically to the retirement age set, covering what I feel are the two most important categories of your life at this point—uncovering your **current personality, behavior, and values.**

Part 1

The Companion Workbook provides worksheets to complete the following Personality and Behavior type exercises. Everyone is a combination of these with one or two aspects that primarily dominate their persona. Before going further in the reading, take some time and fill in the Personality and Behavior test in the workbook.

Your Characteristic Traits Title	Circle adjectives that describe your primary personality traits - what you think of yourself. Put the number circled in the score column				Score (Total words circled)
A	Organized	Dependable	Influence others with data	Predictable	
	Conscientious	Accurate	Careful	Likes to make a plan	
	Reliable	Diplomatic	Stable	Analytical	
	Enjoys old routines	Some say stubborn	Likes to plan ahead	Doesn't like criticism	
B	Spontaneous	New challenges	Risk taker	Meet new people	
	Enthusiastic	Social	Needs variety	Really wants to be liked	
	Easily loses focus	Doesn't need along time	Joins groups	Glass is half full	
	Collaborative	Convincing	Doesn't always follow through	Optimistic	
C	Loves a challenge	A leader	Works hard to excel	Owns flashy things - a show off	
	Wants to be unique	Likes to be admired	Mentors others	Proud of possessions	
	Can be selfish	Doesn't like small talk	Gets things done	Takes the lead in a group	
	Takes control	Bottom line results	Need to win	Low on empathy	
D	Tenacious in goals	Making progress	Perfectionist	Intolerant of the less accomplished	
	Alone time is okay	Can be bored with nothing new	Challenge focused until completed	Studies new challenges	
	Learn new skill for work in retirement	"What can go wrong?" attitude	Bored if mastered a task	Just shows up without reservations	
	Life long learner	Always wants more progress	Always more achievements	Learn new skills	
E	Selfless	Inspiring to others	Work hard toward beliefs	Neglect themselves	
	Modesty	Likes security	Patient	Empathetic	
	Cooperation	Loyal	Doesn't reveal true feelings	Consistent	
	Prone to burnout	Fear of letting others down	Accommodating	Could display more confidence	

Figure 2-1

Gold star for taking the adjective test! Now, what does it all mean? Below is a mini cheat sheet chart. The highest total score for one or two characteristic traits are your highest predominant personality behavior styles.

	Score	Character	Positive	Negative	Descriptor
A		i's Dotted & t's Crossed	Steady	May be boring	Detailed / Reliable
B		Happy Go Lucky	Social	Not content	Variety / Social
C		Master of the Universe	Leader	Big ego	Special / Action
D		Adventurer	The Do'er	Not satisfied	Strive & Grow
E		The Giver	Giving Back	Possibly a pushover	Giving / Peacekeeper

Figure 2-2

The five main character types:

1. **i's Dotted and t's Crossed** – predictable, attention to detail, expects things will unfold as imagined.
2. **Happy Go Lucky** – social, enjoys the feeling of togetherness, and expects that life will serve up its share of changes.
3. **Master of the Universe** – seeks the sense of being admired or unique, the leader.
4. **Adventurer** – achiever, feeds off the feeling that we are making progress.
5. **The Giver** – giving of themselves and believes that everyone is part of something bigger than themselves.

Remember that the results of this test can vary over your lifetime.

You can take the test when you are having a great time in your life and have a lot of confidence in your current relationships and endeavors. Compare that to taking the test a few years later when you may have a few big negatives impacting your life like a serious debilitating disease, a partner passing, or losing friends from different groups you enjoyed. You are still the same core person, but your test numbers may change. This is completely normal. It's normal for your scores to change because, let's face it, your feelings can change on a day-to-day basis.

Now let's get a little more detail for each personality type so you can get an idea of what makes you tick currently.

This system looks at five basic styles which describe how people approach life and relationships and how that can impact your retirement years.

We Are All Unique with A Combination of FIVE Personality and Behavior Characteristics

We are All Individuals

Now that you and hopefully your partner have a better understanding of your personality style from completing the exercises in the previous section, we are going to dig deeper to get a clearer picture of the characteristics that drive us.

It's easy to ignore that we all have different needs, aptitudes, inclinations, and motivations as we follow the herd or try to mold others according to our preconceptions. Here we can get to know ourselves as we make our way in the world so that we can grow to live in retirement and be comfortable with our unique disposition. Many people throughout the centuries have studied human needs. A couple of the most famous of these people are Abraham Maslow and John Burton who both studied human needs psychology. In this book I am presenting an easy-to-understand self-testing program that can give you a ballpark idea of these principles and an opportunity to learn more about yourself and your partner. It's perfect for our purposes here. If you're interested in going deeper, see a list of resources in this book's Index.

The idea is that everybody's actions are driven by the desire to fulfill one or more of five basic human needs. These are characteristics we all share, but everybody is unique, so we do not all value needs equally. Different people will emphasize different needs, and these needs will change throughout a person's life.

The FIVE Personality & Behavior Characteristics

1.   i's Dotted and t's Crossed, Detailed and Reliable

Everybody needs a level of i's dotted and t's crossed attention to detail in their daily lives. If my next meal was not guaranteed, I would probably not be writing this book. I would be worried about survival. If your partner had been rushed to intensive care you would mostly certainly drop everything and do whatever you could to try to help. All these situations threaten our sense of certainty, those things we take for granted that form the bedrock of our lives.

We all have the need for i's Dotted and t's Crossed, but this need can be met in many different ways. Some feel they need a home to be ROUTINE, others need 10 million dollars to be ROUTINE.

I's dotted and t's crossed characters place an emphasis on working conscientiously within existing circumstances to ensure quality and accuracy.

I's dotted and t's crossed styles are motivated by opportunities to gain knowledge, show their expertise, and produce quality work. They prioritize ensuring accuracy, maintaining stability, and challenging assumptions. They are often described as careful, analytical, systematic, diplomatic, accurate, and tactful.

- **Fears:** criticism and being wrong; strong displays of emotion
- **Values:** quality and accuracy
- **Overuses**: analysis, restraint
- **Influences others by** logic, exacting standards
- **In conflict** focuses on logic and objectivity; overpowers with facts
- **Could improve effectiveness through** acknowledging others' feelings, looking beyond data

I's dotted and t's crossed style tend to have goals such as these:

- stick to objective processes
- be accurate and correct
- demonstrate stability and reliability
- attain knowledge and expertise

2. Happy Go Lucky - Variety and Social

Happy Go Lucky characters would use the cliché "Variety is the spice of life," and in life, complete predictability dulls the proverbial taste buds. Imagine being a sports fan and knowing that your team will win every game and every single trophy in their competition. That part of your life would be boring and uninteresting.

We need ROUTINE and VARIETY in our lives. Our need for routine and diversity explains why mainstream Hollywood films remain popular and sustainable. Routine and happy endings are fine things, but we need variety in the plot.

Happy Go Lucky characters are social animals, and we love to be around our fellow humans. The need for relationships is more dominant in women. Of course, men feel this too, but the bonds are innately more potent in the typical woman than the typical man. Men feel more of an immediate connection to others. Women tend to develop relationships more cautiously, though the feelings tend to be stronger and more intimate.

People with a Happy Go Lucky style are enthusiastic, spontaneous, and love to meet new people and take on new challenges. They are social butterflies that flit from person to person and relationship to relationship without becoming disillusioned or losing focus.

Happy Go Lucky characters are motivated by social recognition, group activities, and relationships. They prioritize being active, collaboration, and expressing enthusiasm and are often described as warm, trusting, optimistic, magnetic, enthusiastic, and convincing. They tend to be great team players who are sensitive to the needs of others and supportive partners and parents.

- **Fears:** loss of influence, disapproval, being ignored, and rejection
- **Values:** coaching and counseling, freedom of expression, democratic relationships
- **Overuses:** optimism, praise
- **Influences others through** charm, optimism, energy
- **In conflict** expresses feelings, gossips
- **Could improve effectiveness through** being more objective, following through on tasks

Happy Go Lucky characters tend to have goals such as these:

- attain victory with flair
- pursue friendships and happiness
- achieve status through authority and prestige
- seek approval and be popular
- generate excitement

Happy Go Lucky Quote by Anne Frank:

Whoever is happy will make others happy too.

3. Masters of the Universe: Need to Lead, Feel Special and Excel

Masters of the Universe need to feel special. Of course, we all want to be unique, but some of us protest against that desire. One way to feel special is to build something, like a business, career, philanthropic practice, or family connections.

People whose primary need is to be special can be happy, take leadership positions, work hard, excel in their chosen field and be fearless when faced with challenges. However, they can also be selfish, insensitive to the perspectives of others, and neglect those close to them. Some people feel so comfortable with themselves that they feel bad for those around them who are less satisfied with their lives. These problems can be shared and built through making connections with others.

Masters of the Universe characters tend to place a strong emphasis on shaping the environment and overcoming opposition to accomplish results.

Masters of the Universe characters are motivated by winning, competition, and success. They prioritize taking action, accepting challenges, and achieving results and are often described as direct and demanding, strong-willed, driven, and determined. Masters of the Universe styles tend to be outspoken but can be rather skeptical and questioning of others.

- **Fears:** being seen as vulnerable or being taken advantage of
- **Values:** competency, action, concrete results, personal freedom, and challenges
- **Overuses:** the need to win, resulting in win/lose situations
- **Influences others by** assertiveness, insistence, competition
- **In conflict** speaks up about problems; looks to even the score
- **Could improve effectiveness through** patience, empathy

Styles tend to have goals such as these:

- strive for unique accomplishments
- explore new opportunities

- maintain control of the audience
- achieve independence
- get bottom-line results

Masters of the Universe Quote:

Actions speak louder than words.

4. Adventurer – Strive and Grow

The Greeks taught us that we need a target, something at which to aim our arrows when we try because we are *teleological* beings. We aspire for more; it's never an option to shrink and remain silent.

Imagine you are happy with your life, and it's something you don't want to change. Of course, that's probably never the case, but one can dream. But if it is the case, then retirement would just be more of the same, and you would never have asked yourself the questions that led you to start reading this book.

The greater your dissatisfaction with life, the more your retirement becomes a crisis. The phenomenon is illustrated by the numerous cases of Olympic champions and other elite athletes who achieve their goals and then fall into depression. This is because they have invested so much in one set of goals that help them be a star athlete that they no longer plan to move their lives forward in other areas after they can no longer perform at highly competitive levels.

It is universal that people are happier when they strive and make progress, but it's the progress of striving that counts, not the goal itself. People whose main characteristic is to seek are great students and teachers. They are creative, innovative, and persistent in pursuit of their dreams. But unfortunately, they can also become detached from others, intolerant of the perception of being less powerful and prone to perfectionism.

- **Fears:** stagnation and lack of movement forward
- **Values:** accomplishments and success in goals
- **Overuses:** planning and preparation
- **Influences others by:** being an example
- **In conflict:** is brutally honest
- **Could improve effectiveness through:** patience for other's limitations

Adventurer characters tend to have goals such as these:

- Follow a plan to conclusion
- Punctuality according to plan
- Find the next goal
- Lead a team
- Coach a team for improvement

Adventurer Quote:

> *If you don't have a map,*
> *you'll end up on the wrong road.*

5. The Giver: Giving and Peacekeeper

The Giver character feels deeply that the meals we make for ourselves are uninspiring compared to what we might make for others. That is true for everyone but even more important to the Giver; we all need to step away from our drama.

We all know people do good for others. Young children feel a great sense of contentment when they give.

An example from my life was giving time to my family, especially my mother, in all the stages of my father's Alzheimer's. She cared for him for years to allow him the comforts of home while he was healthy enough. But as his health declined, she made sure he was in a Memory Care home where he was treated well. Then, she would visit him every day to help him with lunch and keep him company. I tried to be there as often as I could. I drove home from those visits feeling warm inside that my connection to my mom was helping to care for my dad.

When my father died, she was able to stop focusing on giving and *give herself* time with the other human characteristics. She gave her time as best she could while my father was alive. My Mom was a very strong Giver character during this time of her life, but now she has changed focus and is now an i's dotted and t's crossed Character.

The Giver's focus is to make the world a better place by using their gifts and talents. Focusing on giving is a great way to combat the depraved human obsession with wealth, fame, beauty, power, and possessions and direct our energy and passion towards more meaningful goals.

The Giver characters tend to place emphasis on cooperating with others within existing circumstances to carry out a task to its best and most rewarding conclusion.

The Giver characters are motivated by cooperation, opportunities to help, and sincere appreciation. They prioritize giving support, collaborating, and maintaining stability and are often described as calm, patient, predictable, deliberate, stable, and consistent.

- **Fears:** change, loss of stability, offending others, letting people down
- **Values:** loyalty, helping others, security
- **Overuses:** modesty, passive resistance, compromise
- **Influences others by** accommodation, consistent performance

- **In conflict** listens to others' perspectives; keeps their own needs to themselves
- **Could improve effectiveness through** displaying more self-confidence, revealing their true feelings

The Giver character tends to have goals such as these:

- cultivate harmony and stability with those in need
- strive to improve personal talents to help others
- find new ways to help others
- give back even before helping themselves
- maintain status quo and control of the environment

Giver Quote:

If everyone pitches in,
we can make sure everyone is taken care of.

Part 2

Discover and Choose Your Core Values

Knowing your values can guide your actions and promote inner peace.

Author Stephen R. Covey states:

"People can't live with change if there's not a changeless core inside them. The key to the ability to change is a changeless sense of who you are, what you are about and what you value."

Your core values tell you what kind of person you want to be. Life offers an endless array of options and choices, large and small, that require you to make difficult choices. Knowledge of your values will guide your actions and give you inner peace. Many people talk about becoming clear about their values and using them as a guideline for life.

A value is an individual belief that people have in things they consider important in their lives. These beliefs are the fundamental motivation for how people act and behave. We cultivate values in our lives, beginning in early childhood.

Although these values differ between individuals, we find shared values in families, cultures, groups, and countries. An example of a common value is patriotism, which is prevalent across borders.

Many family members share similar values because of their upbringing. Like all values, people should be aware of how they value others. Being aware of your core values can be a priceless guide to a life that is meaningful and helps you make the right decisions for yourself. Following one's core values can bring purpose. Conversely, the decision to opt-out of one of these values can create a feeling of distress, discomfort, guilt, and loss.

You maintain your sense of personal responsibility and sense of self-worth. Values are an essential part of your personality and determine how you live your life. Your values evolve throughout your life as your circumstances change, but many remain constant. Discovering your values—the things that matter most to you in life—is a process of self-discovery.

Use your time and energy for things that promote your values. To live a whole life, try spending most of your time doing things consistent with your value system. This practice will ensure that you experience a sense of importance and greater satisfaction with what you do and how you spend your time. However, not all the activities you undertake will match your values.

You need to pay attention to these activities and your feelings. If you do not find meaning in these activities, you won't be fulfilling your values. The feeling that something isn't meaningful is a massive clue from the universe or your inner knowledge that you need to change your activities.

Once you have defined and prioritized your core values, an essential part of the process is using them to guide your life. You will feel better if you live your life by your values. But first, we must learn our deepest core values to live our most fulfilling and meaningful life.

If you are not sure what your core values are or want to clarify which of your values should be your top priority, complete the exercise in the workbook to document the three to six values that mean most to you. It can be helpful to decide (or re-decide) what these values are and abbreviate them.

Choosing Your Core Values

To do this, you need a good list. Look for more words if you like – choices are actually almost endless.

Select your top three to six values. Yes, you can change your mind. In fact, it's natural to modify some of the values on your list as you face new and challenging situations. However, other values represent enduring ideals that you would only change under duress.

List of Values:

Financial Confidence	Connection/Relationships	Creativity	Growth
Compassion	Learning	Assertiveness	Security
Health/Fitness	Leadership	Determination	Love
Nature	Survival	Calmness	Optimisism
Accomplishment	Self-Preservation	Equality	Significance
Dependability	Adventure	Compassions	Strength
Loyalty	Family	Contribution	Trust
Beauty	Work	Courage	Honesty
Bravery	Success	Authenticity	Giving
Gratitude	Freedom	Connection	

Figure 2-3

Understanding Your Core Values

Think of the people you most admire or love. Consider why they are so important to you.

Values can be personified in people that you love and admire. Using your workbook, you can complete a simple two-part process to uncover the values that you associate with your significant others and role models.

Step 1: Identify and write down people who are important role models or valued connections for you.

Step 2: Think of the values they embody. For example, your list might include: "my grandfather for his acceptance and love," "my wife for her honesty," "my friend for his authenticity," and "my brother for his loyalty," to name a few.

Names of People You Admire	Core Values

Figure 2-4

Deepening Your Understanding of Your Core Values

Review the core values you selected for yourself and remember that during self-discovery you are trying to understand who you are today not who you wish to be. Don't put down that you are a learner for a core value if you have not applied yourself to learn, take classes, read, or study anything in 5 years – that is not you at this time. That's called being self-delusional and we all can struggle with this part. Also, no one is perfect so if you told a lie once it doesn't not mean you cannot have honesty as a core value- you are human remember. Compare your selection of core values (Figure 2-3) to the core values of people you admire (Figure 2-4). Now think of what truly guides you and create a list of 3 to 6 core values that define you at this point in time.

Core values can change and evolve over time!

There are times when two values will be in conflict. Knowing why you are choosing Value 1 instead of Value 2 can be helpful in resolving any inner conflict you may feel. And different values may rise to the top in particular situations. For example, during an emergency, "survival" may become the value that guides your actions.

In my financial planning practice, I notice people's values will also shift over time as you fulfill your various goals—for example, once you achieve a comfortable degree of "financial security," that value may recede into the background, and other values may take its place, such as "giving back."

Know Your Values, Know Yourself

Values are one of the key elements to knowing who you are. Values reveal and build character throughout your life as you act on them. Your values are even more important than your goals because you might not reach your goals, but you can almost always choose to live by your values.

> *Your beliefs become your thoughts,*
> *Your thoughts become your words,*
> *Your words become your actions,*
> *Your actions become your habits,*
> *Your habits become your values,*
> *Your values become your destiny.*
> — Gandhi

Know Your Partner

Going back to the workbook, combine the core values that you identified as important to you and your partner along with what you admire in others. Find 3 to 6 values from each of your lists that jump out as your core values.

Core Values for Yourself (list 3-6)	Core Values for Your Partner (list 3-6)

Figure 2-5

Once you and your partner have completed all the exercises in this section of the workbook, it's time to grab a coffee, soda pop, water, wine, craft beer, cocktail, or whatever keeps you engaged and relaxed, and sit and discuss each section with your partner. This conversation is fun and will reveal some surprises. Be patient and understanding. These exercises can bring up unexpected emotions. Be prepared to ride these out. Later in the book, we talk about bucket lists. Understanding your personality, behavior, and values helps uncover bucket list goals you can do together as well as areas that you will either do independently or with others outside of your partnership.

This reflection will also provide you with the tools to understand where you are similar and very different. You can look at ways to understand each other on a better level by looking at what drives you. It's not our job to change each other but to enjoy the similarities and differences.

Understanding our human characteristics can help us know which attributes we should fulfill, which attributes we should abandon, and what are the things we really want so that there is no conflict or trade-off between fulfilling these attributes at the expense of others. This understanding also can help us in our relationships by helping form a complete understanding of factors that motivate other people's actions, attitudes, and abilities before we become judgmental.

Self-assessments and assumptions about what we know about ourselves are never 100% true, of course, but this simple test gives us an idea of the qualities that drive us.

You definitely get a gold star for reading this chapter in detail and completing the workbook by yourself and with your partner.

You and your partner are doing something to impact your life in a very positive way!

Bring these new ideas you learned to each other and discuss them. Not all of your discoveries are going to match up - that is not the point. Don't focus on areas that are conflicting – look at similarities and learn about yourself and learn about your partner. That's how we all grow!

Chapter Three

Connections with Other People

Relationships Can Feed Your Happiness!

We humans are social creatures. Some of us are more social than others. Contrasts between the two can range from the neighbor you've lived next to for twenty years whose name you barely know to the neighborhood snoop who wants to tell you the gory details about people that you'd rather not know and is none of your business. At the office, we tend not to notice just how many people we brush up against during our work life until we find ourselves at home wondering why we feel isolated. Many of us got a dose of that feeling during the COVID-19 pandemic. Even those who aren't social animals felt lonely. But we understood the pandemic wasn't going to go on for three decades. Your retirement may. Loneliness is something you will undoubtedly experience from time to time during your retirement.

Positive social relationships are a MAJOR *Key to Happiness* at any time. They are the sprinkles on the cupcake of life! It is essential to keep developing new relationships and nurturing older ones as we age.

Before You Retire, What Does the Family Think?

There are **THREE CATEGORIES** of people with whom you should maintain close relationships and do your best to deepen those relationships, and it's essential to work on all three. The three categories are:

1. Children and Grandchildren
2. Siblings, Mom and Dad, even Cousins
3. Friends (make new friends and renew old relationships)

The reason it's necessary to work on all three is that some relationships will grow faster than others, some will end up dying off (literally), and some will blossom and grow. Remember, you have 30 years, give or take, of retirement. You don't want to put all your efforts into one best friend or one or two categories because it cuts down your odds of happiness. You don't want to suddenly say, ten years from now, "I should have listened to Ted" because your best friend passed of an untimely illness and your children got divorced, and now your grandchildren are estranged and live five states from you. It's always good to diversify, diversify, *diversify*—you never know what could happen!

Children and Grandchildren

Let's say you are very happy as a grandparent, but then maybe your kids move due to work, or they get divorced, and your connection is cut off. You can 100% count on the fact that kids grow up and begin lives of their own.

Ever know a friend in high school or college who ignored everyone else when they had a steady? Then they broke up, and your friend wanted you to be their best friend instantly. Don't be that grandparent—you will lose your friend group.

Be the grandparent you'd wish for. Not an overbearing know-it-all, but a loving and caring person your grandkids can talk to and enjoy being around. Take time in your retirement to reconnect with your children. But remember, you'll have to do it on their terms. They lead busy lives and have families and children of their own to care for. Take advantage of opportunities to have those conversations you were too busy to have when you lived a more active life. Don't be above a bit of bribery—a trip to Disney would be fun for all. Still, even if you don't have that much money, it's about spending quality time.

Don't Live for Your Kids

One of the biggest financial mistakes older parents are making is deferring their retirement lives to take care of their kids and grandkids—to help them with various expenses, including education, home purchases, and weddings. You have done as any good parent would have, wanting to see their children get a good start in life, but there needs to be a limit.

Older parents will want to be cautious of older children who may begin to believe that they are retiring too. Remember, your kids don't retire with you. You've set a good example. I recommend continuing to do so by planning for yourself. That doesn't mean being ungenerous when it comes time for a wedding or grandchild. It means being careful you don't become seen as an ATM.

AARP reported that in 2019 almost 60% of parents gave $1,000 or more in financial support to their 18–29-year-old. With the pandemic of 2020/21, that number indeed went up. What's of concern isn't $1,000 here and there, especially for an emergency. It's that 25% of respondents to the AARP survey gave over $5,000 to their children in 2019. The zeros add up to serious money. If you're constantly pulling money from your retirement savings, you may be opening the door to delaying retirement and possibly working longer than you'd planned. Who wants to do that if they can avoid it?!

You sacrificed and planned for retirement. Of course, you're thinking about your legacy and your family's future. Perhaps part of your wealth is inherited, and you feel a responsibility to protect it for future generations. That's all well and good, but right now it's yours. It's there for your lifetime and for your needs and desires. Retirement is a stage of life, and it has its own costs, awareness of impending mortality among them. You need to spend these years having the experiences you didn't have time for while working and raising a family.

Remember the stages we talked about? It's important to get in the more physically demanding activities while you are healthy.

Expect Expectations to Change in Retirement

Retirement is here and you want to celebrate the event. So, what do you do? You decide to take the family to Europe for the summer. You'll rent first-class train cabins and the whole family will practice French and Italian together throughout countless bistros and five-star restaurants. They'll love it. Right?

But your kids have already deposited thousands of dollars on summer camps and clubs for their kids. Their summer vacations are already planned, and you soon learn that your kids have their own ideas about how you'll be spending retirement.

In reality you might be surprised just how many different retirement plans have been formulated *for you* by family members *other than you* (i.e., your grown children). Until you communicate your goals with them, everyone will end up adjusting expectations.

Yes, it's your retirement, and just like with your choice of career, such as where you worked and the stress of your job, your decisions will affect the people you care for the most. The fact is, when your plans impact the lives of your grown children, siblings, maybe even your own parents, it's important to share with them what you're thinking about doing and buying. Your adult children have their own family goals, routines, and time management practices. When you want to do something with them or for them, the first discussion should be how your plans and theirs can run on parallel tracks.

Your grown children may not be able to meet your schedule. They could be juggling endless extracurricular activities for your grandchildren and hard-pressed to fit in more activities. No matter how wonderful the potential train trip across Europe, the reality of what's needed next school year is dominating their family plans.

I know, it's amazing the downtime we got just by buying our kids' bikes. But our adult children feel a need to participate more closely in their kids' activities. Good or bad, who's to say, but we can expect to run into some baffling overplanning on the part of our grown kids. It's our job to include them according to their needs and plans.

Gather Input and Avoid Assumptions

If you'd like to offer an extended family vacation or a sailboat that you can all enjoy, talk to your loved ones and be ready for a variety of responses.

Having conversations before making a personal or financial commitment allows for more balanced input from both sides, rather than approaching the conversation from the position of already having made a down payment.

It will allow your children the opportunity to share their thoughts honestly without moving them to consider the impact they will have on actions you've already taken.

Then, give each of your children time and space to think about it, and be prepared that they might not receive your proposal as you had hoped.

Be open to whatever your kids propose, take some time to consider it, and give them your honest response.

You may come up with something fun that hadn't been part of the original discussion. By being open about your plans and expectations, you will strengthen family relationships at the beginning of your retirement.

You might conclude that it would be better to travel to interesting places for holidays when everyone can more easily schedule time together.

Communicate Honestly

You might make personal interests a priority in your retirement. You might want to spend your free time playing golf or becoming a woodcrafter. Maybe you plan to do it all.

But your grown children may have plans for *you*. They might be thinking how great it'd be for you to babysit regularly. Here again, communicate what you want, even about the obvious. Of course, you want to see your grandkids. No, you're not a babysitting service.

Suppose you start babysitting because you want to avoid feeling uncomfortable. In that case, you're stuck unless you want to doubly upset your grown kids by telling them you only agreed because you wanted to avoid conflict. Clarify expectations early before feelings get hurt. Honest communication includes defining what you *will* do, not just stating what you will not do.

Embrace Your Retirement

It's exciting to think of a retirement that will go on for dozens of years — doing the things you want to do with your loved ones. You have more time left than one would have expected a century ago. Once upon a time, you'd be just about at the end of your road. Retirement is a relatively modern concept.

Back in the early 1900s, the average parent lived about two years after their last child left home. When Social Security was just getting started, that life expectancy had grown to five years past the last child leaving home.

And ultimately, you might even decide that you want to travel Europe without your extended family. After all, traveling on your own can open up many adventures.

Siblings, Mom and Dad, Even Cousins

Perhaps you've been estranged from a family member. Yes, I know, we can pick our friends but not our family. But regardless of what has happened over the years, you can often rekindle these relationships late in life in significant ways.

Have you lost touch with a sibling? It's surprising how time and age can mend old wounds—make the phone call. I suggest you and your sibling get together without spouses to instigate a renewed connection.

What is the benefit of reconnecting? As we get older, brothers and sisters become the people we've known and shared the most history, especially once parents and close relatives from their generation start to pass. A lot of time is still on the clock as we approach retirement. Even the bitterest disagreements and resentments will give way as old age draws near. The sooner you reach out, the sooner you and your siblings can regrow ties. As we pull into retirement age, siblings will be experiencing many of the burdens and the joys of the closing act of our lives, the same as you.

When we're toddlers, brothers, sisters, and the dog are the first creatures we encounter about the same size as us. We have no choice but to intermingle with them. But a significant change happens after the teenage years. Siblings drift off to go to college, take jobs, get married, and have kids of their own. As a result, we see our siblings outside of family functions less often as our life paths diverge. We find ourselves at different stages of life with different priorities.

As our children grow up, grandchildren arrive, and our parents begin to enter advanced age, lives change course. Our siblings are experiencing the exact same thing. If we don't come together first for another reason, we'll be talking one day, after many years about needing to discuss and agree on care for our aged parents. Maybe, one day, we'll be making palliative care decisions for each other.

Siblings will be there to play the part that's needed most. Siblings will do things that are almost too much to ask of a friend. Ask yourself, if your estranged sibling reached out to you for help, what would you do?

Time runs out on the midlife family stage. You only have so much time. Likewise, the curtain closes eventually. Death stalks the cast and will pick off the characters one by one. Vulnerable to that drawn curtain, midlife siblings need to resolve brother and sister breaches before a chronic illness, or sudden death takes a sibling and leaves behind nothing but regret.

Brothers and sisters will come through for us in a million ways. A person to laugh with over something personal or a shoulder to cry on. They can share the stress of making tough decisions. When we retire with sheet cakes and champagne, the biggest toasters can be siblings.

When parents are making their move into an assisted living community, likely it'll be your job to sort out the collected furniture and decades of junk. Siblings have a stake in this too and turns out this is a move that's hard for everyone. You may be losing the home where you and your siblings grew up. You may be confronted with boxes of board games you used to play every weekend. You will find memorabilia that will bring about strong emotions, both good and bad. However, you can share these moments with siblings and make them special.

Brothers and sisters are among the first people we can call in a health care crisis. If we become disabled or are ill, that sibling air mattress will reinflate on a dime, and they'll do everything from going on the web to find resources to coming to our home and nursing us back to health.

Why burden yourself with getting through the past before you can enjoy nostalgia and the love of your entire family? Get over the past mishaps now. *Sooner* is a good time to re-establish and build connections.

Friends (make new friends and rekindle old relationships)

Often, this is about reconnecting with college or high school classmates, past neighborhood friends, and even past co-workers!

Define What a "Friend" Is to You

What do you value most in your friends? For example, do you look for people who enjoy the same activities as you? Do you like spending time with people who share similar beliefs? Or do you prefer acquaintances that challenge your assumptions and make you think—I laugh as I write that last line. Does anyone like to be challenged and participate in discourse anymore? Debate is something we tend to avoid so everyone can just get along.

First, and most obvious, when you know what kinds of friends you are looking for, you can choose to engage in activities that will allow you to meet new people of your choosing. For example, are there political, religious, sports, social, or other groups through which you can reengage?

Second, taking the time to think about what friendship means to you will make it more likely that you will see opportunities to start conversations in more natural settings, like at the supermarket, in the post office, or the park.

Give some thought to what you're looking for in a friend. Write your thoughts and impressions in a diary if you have time. Friendship takes time, effort, and planning. Think about the type of person that you'd like to meet, and you just might increase your chances of meeting them!

Start with Your Existing Social Network – But Don't Limit Yourself to It

One of the most rewarding ways to build new relationships is to reconnect with your old friends from high school, college, or work. Of course, most people change over time. Sometimes, the people that you had a lot in common with when you were younger have changed, and you don't have so much in common with them anymore. Other people who you may not have liked very much now seem more like you.

You might be surprised that you have developed divergent interests with your old friends in the years after school. Or you might find that you can pick up where you left off with an old friend who drifted away.

If you don't want to pick up the phone right away, there's always social media. You can renew and maintain your friendship from a distance to start.

The first few times you reach out will be the hardest. The more people you can connect with, the easier it will be to find other long-lost friends. Your old friends are many times in the same boat and probably would appreciate the call from an old friend!

Even if it feels funny at first, don't let your apprehension hold you back. Yes, people are busy, and you may not get a response. But, if you reach out to several, some of your old friends will get back to you.

People almost always like to stay connected, and you never know where a renewed contact will take you.

Embrace Your Passions Instead of Chasing New Relationships

One of the fantastic things about being 60 is that we finally know what we want. We understand our values and understand what we want to accomplish in our lives.

If you are like many folks over 60, you may have a feeling that, with less time in front of you than behind, it's time to focus on adding people to your life that share your passions and dreams. This is one of the reasons that your passions, interests, and skills can be such a great friendship resource.

What are you passionate about? Do you have a favorite hobby like gardening, chess, knitting, tennis, golf, writing, cooking, or reading? Do you have any special skills that other people might be interested in learning?

While you are exploring, don't feel limited to meeting people your own age. Be open to connecting with people of all ages! Some of the strongest friendships that I have are with people decades younger than me.

Don't be afraid to connect with strangers when you attend an event, club, or activity. One of the ironies of social events is that everyone tends to think that they are the only one that is nervous to talk to others. A hint for you that I find interesting is to not leave immediately when the activity ends. Stick around and see who stays for some small talk. Also, when you attend events get there a little early and catch some small talk before the big crowd shows up. If you want a reason for getting there early or leaving late, ask to help set up or take down. You'll make friends pitching in for sure!

Talking to new people can be scary, but don't fear taking a chance on strangers. If you are in a public place, the worst that can happen is someone might not be who you are looking for in a friend.

Despite everything we know about the importance of maintaining social connections as we get older, finding friends after 60 can be a challenge. As we age, the easy social relationships we built as schoolmates, parents, and colleagues change. When my three kids were in little league, our community had a local park with four baseball fields connected by a snack concession stand in the middle. Those Saturday mornings were the highlight of my week because not only was I watching my kids play ball, but all the dads from their school and neighborhood were there. We yucked it up telling stories and laughing. I really enjoyed all of my children's sporting activities for both of those reasons.

New people in the neighborhood can also be a source of new friendships.

Four Easy Ways to Make New Friends

So, now you know the terrible news. However, there's a more important lesson here, and that's what you can do to combat isolation. The good news is there are plenty of options when it comes to making new friends and having new experiences. Here are four easy ideas (with more to come in the "Bucket List" sections of the next chapter).

Join a Club

Probably one of the top ways to make long-lasting friends is to join a club. That's where you'll meet lots of people who share a common interest. Clubs exist for that very reason, and they also provide a platform for showing your expertise. Sharing what you're good at is a beautiful way to build rapport with club members.

You don't have to be an expert at something to make new friends, however. Joining a club to learn something new is an excellent way to meet people, too. According to studies, socializing also keeps the brain active and healthy, which is a perfect way to help ward off mental decline and even dementia.

Joining a club or picking up a hobby may sound like a small change, but it could make all the difference. A quick Google search will return many articles where you can learn about the importance of hobbies in retirement.

Volunteer

Consider giving back during your retirement. See what's going on in your church, community or other charitable organizations. Local hospitals often need seniors for concierge volunteer work. Local preschools look for seniors to help with one-on-one reading skills. If you want to travel, there are many overseas opportunities as well.

Donating your time and your experience is a way to make friends and make a difference in the world while you're at it. Whether you volunteer at the hospital, local literacy program, or soup kitchen doesn't matter as long as it's a rewarding way of spending your time during retirement. There are limitless ways to volunteer, so you're bound to find a volunteer project that excites you.

Join a Community Center

Social opportunities abound at community centers that serve as hubs for people to socialize, volunteer, take classes, and participate in physical fitness programs. If you happen to retire to an active adult community, you're ready to go because a community center is an integral part of most residential communities for seniors. But if you live in an independent home, check with your local senior center, your church, or the town hall for ideas.

Joining a community center can be a life-changing experience for some adults, particularly one based on faith. Whether you grew up in a faith-based household or are looking for a spiritual outlet, a faith-based community may be just what you need.

Consider Mentoring

Would you like to stay in touch with the industry where you built your career? If you don't want to teach before a group, find a young person to mentor. Take time out of your week to change the life of someone else. Many young people would love the chance to learn from experienced and successful people.

Mentoring consists of sharing your knowledge with younger people in your field. It has the added benefit of offering retirees a meaningful way to interact with younger generations—something found to be increasingly difficult as decades go by.

Mentoring doesn't just mean helping someone on their career path; it can be as simple as taking a more active role in the lives of your grandchildren. Read this list of inter-generational bonding activities for grandparents and grandchildren.

New Places, New People

At this point, you've developed a basic list of dos and don'ts, communicated your needs and expectations to those close to you, and built a new network of post-work friends and acquaintances.

Stocking your retirement toolkit with a new social acumen makes travel or moving to a new community a simpler experience. You'll know how to meet people and look forward to new neighbors and first meetings with community groups. When you travel, you'll find yourself more easily conversing with locals.

There's a big wide world out there waiting to be explored. If you are looking for new surroundings, temporary or permanent, the options are many.

Using your companion workbook, take some time to evaluate your current relationships. Give yourself a grade of A, B, C, D, or F for each square.

Your Family Group	I'm happy with my current connections	I'm happy with my recent efforts to connect	I want to do more to develop deeper connections	Forgiveness is needed to grow this area	Am I willing to do what it takes to mend this if it's a broken area? Yes, No, Maybe, NA	Number of Close Friends	Number of Casual Associates
Children & Grandchildren							
Mom & Dad							
Silblings							
Cousins							

Figure 3-1

Friend group examples can be neighbors, work, hobby, high school/childhood, college, etc.

Your Current Friend Group	I'm happy with my current connections	I'm happy with my recent efforts to connect	I want to do more to develop deeper connections	Forgiveness is needed to grow this area	Am I willing to do what it takes to mend this if it's a broken area? Yes, No, Maybe, NA	Number of Close Friends	Number of Casual Associates

Figure 3-2

Shared group examples: neighbors, work, hobby, high school/childhood, college, faith, etc.

You & Your Partner's Friend Group	I'm happy with my current connections	I'm happy with my recent efforts to connect	I want to do more to develop deeper connections	Forgiveness is needed to grow this area	Am I willing to do what it takes to mend this if it's a broken area? Yes, No, Maybe, NA	Number of Close Friends	Number of Casual Associates

Figure 3-3

Question:

If you were getting married tomorrow and needed to ask five people to be in your wedding party - would it be easy for you? Would they be surprised to be asked? Who would they be?

List name and group name.

Your List:

1.

2.

3.

4.

5.

Your Partners List:

1.

2.

3.

4.

5.

Chapter Four

What's In You? – A New Kind of Bucket List

Your Social Relationships Impact Your Bucket list

Your financial confidence is the heart of your retirement, but a heart isn't functional without a body to go with it. A heart's purpose is to send blood to other organs. So, if your retirement planning has focused solely on financial security, you may have a tremendously solid financial heart. But you've been considering only one element of what you can view as a more considerable need for security. Indeed, your retirement is incomplete until you actually do something with it.

Now, what do I mean by that?

Think about the pandemic for a second. After more than a year of varying isolation levels, I think we all have some clarity about the mental and physical stress of loneliness and being in close quarters with the same people day after day, even if they are people we love dearly. It's not easy, and it's not healthy for a person or family to live an isolated life.

The primary purpose of our retirement should be to create ways to form and enhance meaningful relationships. That's where we build genuine security. Just like the accomplishments you achieved when you were in school or during your career, you'll enjoy your bucket list accomplishments more when you can share them with friends. Fellow classmates, teammates, and coworkers from the past who are about your same age may be joining you in the retirement world around the same time. Reaching out to them can help give you experience comparisons. In a way, that brings a little bit of your old social order into retirement.

While we often worry about the financial capital we need to retire, few of us consider social capital—the friends we need to stay connected, engaged, fun, and overcome the many challenges that aging brings.

Without a concerted effort to continue discovering new places and activities, meeting new people, renewing old friendships, we face a faster decline in well-being as we age.

Change is a part of retirement. You'll change too, and that makes forging new relationships a little more stressful, perhaps to the point of wanting to withdraw, which I've seen happen.

Realize Two Distinctions: Your Personal Bucket Goals, and Bucket Goals with Your Partner

My wife and I were driving to see a close friend this summer and we tried listening to an audiobook, but it was not something that caught and maintained our attention. So, on our five-hour trip from Chicago to Cleveland, my wife was forced to talk to me about this book. She knows I love to give examples, so she gave me a brilliant one. There is a three-lane highway we are driving on in our marriage. The right lane is MY lane, the left lane is HER lane, and the middle lane is OUR lane. So, as we head into retirement, if we want to grow closer in our relationship, we need to make sure we spend time in all three lanes. Maybe it just happens naturally and works out great for some marriages but not mine. We needed to plan. So, for example, if I want to go on a rustic outdoor camping trip and my wife doesn't, this fits into MY lane and I may do that with the guys. On the other hand, my wife and I both enjoy playing tennis, biking, and boating together so those fit into OUR lane. As you go through your bucket list, include your partner, and look for things for each of your individual lanes while also finding things in the shared lane. Make room for both of these activities.

Because I've learned what drives my partner's personality, behaviors, and her core values, we find that OUR lane is easy and more enjoyable. We are both still big believers in the MY lane time as well, so the tricky part of the journey is figuring out how much time to spend in MY/HER lane vs. OUR lane.

It is at the beginning of any journey of self-discovery you ask yourself: What do I want?

And there's an excellent reason for asking this question that has nothing to do with money or the acquisition of stuff. It's because the very next question you're likely to ask yourself, especially during the early years of retirement, is: Why do I want what I want?

Why Do We Want the Things We Want?

When we were young, we all felt a spark of uniqueness that led us to do many strange things to express ourselves. But, when you think about it, if we are all so unique, aren't we conforming to uniqueness? That was a rhetorical question, of course.

Desires are something we don't control. We assume we want something for a good reason. It might be a necessity. It might be the key to happiness. When we want something, we think that we want it because we believe that in some way, it benefits us.

Sometimes what we want and why we think it's good for us has nothing to do with the object of our desire. For example, we might wish to and be able to afford one kind of car but choose another for practical purposes. And I'm not even talking about better gas mileage.

Think about the person who wants and can afford a Ferrari but chooses a Mercedes AMG because he wants his car to sit appropriately in line in the company parking lot with the other AMGs, flanked by directors' more expensive AMGs.

Some forms of social pressure are ubiquitous and annoying but do little harm. For example, children's fashion and fads reach into our bank accounts (or our parents' accounts when we were kids) as parents, and even (hopefully, as the source of last resort) as grandparents.

Social pressure plagues us so much throughout our lives that we end up used to it. As a result, we may have become dependent on doing what everyone else is doing because it leaves us with fewer questions to answer on our own. We know what we have to do to be a part of something, and we do it. So how about when we retire and are free from being required to be a part of anything?

A Stanford social psychologist, Dr. Leon Festinger, formulated Social Comparison Theory in the 1950s and based it on prior research into communication, dynamics, behavior, and aspirations within social groups. Social Comparison Theory argues that individuals use comparisons with others to gain accurate self-evaluations. Thus, we learn how to define ourselves by comparing ourselves with others.

When a parent lectures their children on not succumbing to peer pressure, the speeches usually sound the same, taken as they are from oft-repeated tropes from the Internet, television, and magazines.

Perhaps, while you were saying them, your kids pointed out, colorfully, that your words about peer pressure sounded trite. It's not hard to understand why that might be the case. Sitting in the family room, the captive teen listens to their parents lecture them about not following the crowd while surrounded by technology, furniture, and art—representing status and conformity.

When we were children, our parents chose our social groups. Then we chose our own friends at school and work, and through it all, there's a combination of choice, chance, coercion, and determination.

However, once retired, every group becomes an option. There are no more imposed groups. Herein lies the danger of loneliness.

The fact is that being part of a group, whether voluntary or not, provides us with a needed sense of community. And as adults, we make compromises in our choice of work, geography, and even family members. You may have found the perfect life partner, but how about their parents, or even your kids. You didn't get to choose those. Your grown grandchildren may create designer children one day, but you did it the old-fashioned way. You rolled the dice and discovered your children as they grew up and ways to love them more and less throughout the years—hopefully more than less.

The innate human desire to belong means that we feel something missing when we aren't part of a group. In our short-term planning, we think more on a social level, and when we plan for retirement, we focus on the finances. In pre-retirement, we measure much of our accomplishments through projects for work, the fruition of community plans, and goals for the family. So much of it comes with a road map. Unfortunately, there's no standard road map for retirement precisely because it is a zone without much social pressure. Hopefully, you're now prepared to create your own map with an understanding of the realities of the road. Retirement's better that way.

Your Bucket List

Perhaps you've begun a Bucket List or completed one, but that was years ago. Much of which has changed. Maybe you thought you'd spend a few years in an RV or travel to the Great Wall of China. Is that what you still want to do?

If you have one to three big things that you have anticipated for years, and you know those aren't going to change, start the list now. Of course, you don't have to have your entire list done before you start. Instead, begin asking around about different tours of China or look into what today's RVs offer.

Maybe you spent time roaming in a van when you were younger or camping in a tent with a sleeping bag on the ground. You know your body wouldn't enjoy that challenge now. A Chevy van with a waterbed may have been paradise when you were young, but you and a companion will need all the space and comforts of home, and RVs come with more options than many homes. So, start looking at models and features early. RVing and long trips are for the early years while you are likely the healthiest that you'll be during retirement.

Not every item on the list has to be a unique, fantastic Instagram-viral experience. One thing might be to teach Sunday School at your church. Another might be to run a 5k.

Everyone is different, and everyone has to figure it out for themselves. Your dreams are your own. How to turn them into goals is a different situation. But, like our work lives, we sometimes need to reach out and accept help to meet our goals.

If you find yourself staring at a blank piece of paper, unable to make your first Bucket List, you can take heart that your partner probably has something in mind to consider doing together. Also, there are friends on this road already. Friends, family, and former co-workers who are now retired are usually happy to help you form a clear picture of what you want to do and how to accomplish your retirement goals. Grabbing lunch or dinner and discussing Bucket List ideas with another couple who may be in your retirement ballpark usually gets the ideas flowing for all of you!

Bucket List items fall into two categories:

A. Goals
B. Experiences

Once you're retired, you'll have more of an independent life. Hopefully, your children have grown and successfully launched into their own orbit.

A common mistake is to spend 90% of your time planning Experience projects and 10% on Goals.

So, what are Goals and Experiences? An example of a Goal would be learning to fly a plane. An example of an Experience would be skydiving.

Skydiving is typically a once or twice thing. Sure, maybe you love it and incorporate jumping out of a plane into your regular plans. But for most retiree skydivers, it's a one and done.

Learning to fly is a commitment. A student pilot must log 40 hours, 20 of them with an instructor. Depending on your time and financial commitment, it can take two months to a year to get a pilot's license.

Then, you'll want to do something with that license. You'll either be renting or purchasing a plane.

That's what's meant by Goals and Experiences. Pre-retirement is full of dreams of flying through the air, climbing mountains and sipping wine in far-away places. And those things are great, and you should plan for them.

But let's get back to that pilot's license for a minute. An entire continent suddenly becomes available to you in a way it wasn't before. Uncanny but exciting places that you wouldn't bother driving to are a few hours away by plane.

Here's a Hollywood story as an example. The actor Harrison Ford is an enthusiastic pilot and lover of good hamburgers. So back in the 80s and 90s, he was known to fly his plane from Malibu to the middle of the California desert for lunch, to an old roadside motel, café, and gas station named Roy's, because they made, in his opinion, the best hamburger in the world. Plus, an old landing strip from the WWII era sat across the street.

If you ever came to California via Route 66 back in the day, Roy's was the first sign of life before the southern California sprawl. Fortunately, after decades of post-interstate decay, Roy's has been undergoing a painstaking restoration over the last five years. The gas station and café are now open, and private planes often outnumber automobiles in the café's parking lot.

America is still full of places that touch on our history. Sometimes they don't have to be open for business. The abandoned Roy's is still a must-stop for Route 66 enthusiasts. These are challenging places to get to by car, or at least inconvenient. They're much more readily available by private plane.

My point is that some good places take time and detective work to find. If you want to skydive, you go on the Internet, type "skydiving school near me," and Google does the rest. Learning to fly a small plane, locating destinations, and planning a trip takes more time.

The Goal projects tend to be the most fulfilling. So, balance your planning time between thinking and planning for the things you'll want to make a fixture in your retirement life and the particular, usually adrenaline-related, stuff you want to experience.

Bucket List Ideas

Because you likely have more time on your hands and better health than you realize, less than you may think is needed to do everything you imagine yourself doing. We've all had the experience of looking back at ourselves five years ago and thinking, "Wow, I thought I was old then, but I was stronger and fitter than I thought I was at the time."

So do not underestimate yourself and your abilities at any stage of retirement.

Developing a Bucket List for each stage of your retirement is sound advice. For example, you might not want to think about senior living communities right now, but if your health stays good, you'll walk tall past most of the other residents as they park their walkers outside the community dining room.

Senior living communities typically offer more than 50 clubs or groups that residents can join for just about every activity imaginable.

If you need to jar your imagination for your list, think of traveling. Where would you like to travel, not only where but how? Meaning airplane, motorcycle, railroad, car, camper, motorhome, bicycle, cruise line, or sailboat. With each of these ideas, getting there can be half the fun. Think back to what you enjoyed in your youth, singing in a choir, musical instruments, stamps, coins, model railroads, or a model racecar. Some of these on your list can be expensive, but they are all things designed to bring joy. Remember these hobbies can be even more fun when you enjoy them with people of like interests.

A Sample of Things to Do When You Retire

Move to the Country

Many retirees consider moving to the country for open space, privacy, and intimate community. Pleasure in retirement can mean staying put, chatting with the same neighbors every day (but being able to retreat to seclusion), cheering for the same local sports teams, and shopping at local retail stores.

Move to the City

City centers are being revitalized and urban areas are becoming fun places to live, especially if you're not ready for a quiet life. If you want all of life's necessities within a few city blocks, move to the city. Downsize your home and become an active member of the metropolis, where you'll get to experience the best of art and culture.

Move out of the Country

Retirement abroad can bring exciting new experiences, change scenery, and a lower cost of living. Retirees often find everything they need, including good weather, cultural attractions, affordable housing, and recreation, in a whole new country. If you are considering retirement abroad, it's a good idea to arrange extended stays of at least a few months in your chosen locations to ensure that your find the right fit (a good vacation destination is not necessarily a good place to live).

A new country can help you see retirement as the beginning of an exciting new phase in your life rather than the end of your productive existence. Retirement abroad can be an exhilarating challenge to develop language skills, learn a new culture, and make friends with a wide variety of people.

Visit Family and Friends

People who keep in touch with family members and friends are on average almost twice as likely to say they would be well prepared for a family problem if faced with one. In most cases, the family makes retirement life more rewarding and enjoyable. However, while some retirees like to spend time at home and visit family and friends, others want a bolder lifestyle.

So, if you are planning an extended adventure, you might want to spend time visiting family first. Renting a house may seem crazy to those who have owned a home. Still, if you have relatives and family friends living in a specific location, a short-term rental offers a relaxed way of making yourself accessible to your extended family.

Start a Business

Sometimes people start a retirement business to provide emotional as well as financial benefits. Whether you are applying your wisdom, experience, common sense, or a combination of the three, a retirement business can be a great way to do what you love while earning income to supplement your retirement savings.

Having your own business can allow you to enjoy much-needed interactions with others. The idea is not to work 40-50 hours a week in a new venture, but to keep active and busy, not overworked, or unhappy. You don't need to go crazy with your new business idea— simply enjoy a feeling of satisfaction while lightening the load on your nest egg.

Get a Part-Time Job

Do you still want a place to go every day but not the day-to-day pressure or stress of running your own business? Taking a fun part-time job doing something that you love may be a suitable happy medium.

A part-time environment that is low stress ideally should keep you moving physically and challenge you mentally. Your part-time employment should not involve repetitive movement; instead, choose light-duty variable activities that do not put too much physical strain on your body.

The extra income a job brings isn't the point. The opportunities for social interaction are abundant in most job environments, and coming from a unique perspective, as a retiree, you have a lifetime of work experience, wisdom, and experience to offer. Plus, surprising positive intergenerational work friendships are a great byproduct of a part-time job.

Be a Mentor

If you want to keep the skills you've used regularly throughout your career, you might want to consider mentoring a newcomer to your previous industry. In addition to sharing lessons learned through your career, you can also act as a soundboard for your student as they take on new challenges. As a mentor, you can be a positive role model in a young person's life and share stories, ideas, fun activities, and challenges without judgment. Among the best ways to give your retirement purpose is to volunteer your time, effort, and experience to another (often younger) person who can benefit from your intuition and knowledge.

Community Volunteering

Volunteering in retirement can improve your quality of life. According to an article for Senior Community Services, participants aged 60 and older who volunteered reported lower disability levels and higher levels of general well-being than those who did not volunteer.

There are many places in our communities where retired volunteers are needed and welcome. Local charities provide opportunities for older volunteers and can be an essential source of information about other volunteering opportunities available in your area.

Teach

Use your hard-earned wisdom and experience to teach others. Many communities would welcome you sharing your technical, life, and professional knowledge. Or perhaps something as easy as a free course at your local library, community center, retirement center, or adult learning hub. You might consider teaching at a local community college or university if you have the qualifications. If not, you could go back to school.

Go into Public Service

Serve your community by participating in the political process. You've got a town council if you're a rural dweller, and numerous commissions if you live in a city. School Boards for K-12 and local community colleges offer an opportunity to give back without disrupting too much retirement fun. If you want to protect your retirement time but still feel that getting involved will do you some good, your homeowner's association is probably the least time-consuming political entity.

Continue Your Education

Did you leave school before you finished a degree? Go back to school, complete your diploma, or get a graduate degree. You can even take classes just for fun, or to learn or improve a language or other skill. Many colleges offer discounts to retirees above certain ages and award credits for life and professional experience.

Read

Spend your days reading all of the books you never had time for. Aim to read all the classics or join a book club and add a social element to your passion.

Write a Book

Writing a book takes time. Now you have plenty of it. Write a novel, a cookbook, a how-to guide, or even your memoirs.

Start a Blog

Blogs aren't just for websites anymore. The meaning of the term has stretched to include pretty much any long-form content published on social media. Platforms like Facebook/Meta and Medium are places designed for posting content of several hundred or even a thousand words. It's the perfect place to keep a running commentary of your retirement and allow others to participate. Lots of other options exist as well. Instagram is a good choice for posting images.

Gardening

As retirement age approaches, most people who enjoy gardening will want to retire to a place where the climate is a good fit. A sunny summer with good rainfall and warm evenings promotes good plant growth, and these are the conditions you need to consider if a gardener is going to retire in the near future. The ideal retreat for gardeners is any place where space is adequate, and the climate supports the garden you want to create.

Learn a New Language

While you may be dreaming of long afternoon walks on exotic beaches and evenings of international fine dining, you'll find the experience more immersive if you speak some local language. Sure, lots of people around the world speak English, and usually a few other languages too. From time to time, you'll also find that you get better service and people may be more friendly to you when you speak the native language.

Learn to Play Music

Still got your Doobie Brothers records? Never have mastered Eddie Van Halen's fret tapping style? Learn or extend your knowledge of the guitar, piano, or other favorite instruments. You'll impress your family at the next get-together with your new musical talent. You can always rent a musical instrument or buy a used one. I recommend real in-person lessons to get started. There are many online lessons, but an in-person commitment may get you to really practice—the key to mastery! Give it a go!

Start a New Hobby

You've got the time to learn new things and expand your interests. Sure, collecting is a possibility, and collectors love to have meetups. Plus, new categories of collectibles are emerging. Are you an engineer who has nostalgia for your old Apple II or Commodore? Vintage tech collecting is big with Millennials and Zoomers. Finding and fixing up old tech and selling it online is an opportunity to build a fun hobby business.

Lots of options like that exist.

Take up a New Sport

Stay active by taking on the challenge of a new athletic pursuit, and I'm not talking about shuffleboard. Take swim lessons, play tennis or racquetball. Many people complete marathons or snow ski well into their retirement.

Join a Fitness Group

Yoga or Tai Chi in the park, accountability works best in groups. Apps are easy to ignore. By being part of a team of people who are looking for accountability toward their fitness goals, it's hard to forget your responsibility in the effort. Work toward getting in the best shape of your life.

Are you inspired? Spend some time in the companion workbook developing your Bucket List. And don't forget to include your partner as you plan your trip down the three-lane highway of retirement!

Priority (A, B, C)	Bucket Items	Goals (G) or Experience (E)	Three Lane Highway		
			MY Bucket List	OUR Bucket List	YOUR Bucket List
	Top 3 to do ASAP				
	Exp. Learn a new language	G		X	
	1.				
	2.				
	3.				
	Misc. Items to Brainstorm				
	1				
	2				
	3				
	4				
	5				
	6				
	7				
	8				
	9				
	10				

Figure 4-1

Please download the Free Companion workbook at www.TedBuckley.com. Additional worksheets and updates are included.

Chapter Five

How To Set and Achieve Big Bucket List Goals

You have just created or reviewed your Bucket List in the previous chapter. The question you're probably asking yourself is, "How am I going to actually complete any of the items on my Bucket List?" This chapter is the pathway to checking off items on your Bucket List goals. In previous chapters, you have hopefully learned many things about yourself, your partner, and what makes you tick, and what Bucket List goals and experiences really interest you. We have so much to do, but do we have the necessary tools to transform desire into action? This chapter is about how to reach those big Bucket List goals.

If you're nearing retirement, you can probably see that you've lived 2/3 of your life up to this point. What have you learned from it? I asked my wife what decade of her life she liked the most. Ages 10 to 20 is a popular response. It's adolescence, early college, and adulthood all in one ten-year swoop. We agreed we loved the child-raising years of 30 to 40 years old. But when we broke our lives down by 10-year segments, ours ebbed and flowed with good decades and not-so-good decades.

So, to give us a chance to make retirement the very best decades of our lives we should probably get some oars in the water and give our journey some direction. Floating down the stream can get us there but when we have a guide and a couple of oars, we can avoid getting stuck on rocks. We are more easily kept on track.

In our retirement years we are looking for happiness and fulfillment. We each have our own definition to what that means, but we are all on a journey. We are going to discuss ways to get up to a higher level on the ladder of happiness through the achievement of goals— REPEATABLE ways to get you to accomplish your Bucket List goals.

But first, we are going to make sure that you are climbing up a ladder that's against the right house. You don't want to climb up a ladder on the wrong house. Imagine climbing the wrong ladder and spending an afternoon cleaning your neighbor's gutters instead of your own. Picking the right tasks to reach the right goal is key.

The accumulation of YOUR CHOICES and DECISIONS have combined to create your entire life up to this moment, BOTH the GOOD and the BAD.

Examples include life-long habits. For example, someone who has been dedicated to a healthy diet and exercise plan since their 20s will have wellness benefits long into retirement. But don't get discouraged if that's not you. You can make choices today that start having an impact for your health right away. You can be 60 years old and start exercising and watching what you eat. Those changes will quickly

impact your energy level and even possibly lower your high blood pressure and improve your A1C. But patterns need to be given time to become ingrained and old patterns need to be unlearned. It takes repetition.

Why are Worthwhile Goals so Difficult to Find and Accomplish?

The first reason is that it's just hard to change a pattern in your life overnight. Another reason is when we were in our 20s and 30s we cherry-picked the easy goals—sales rep, top producing rep, then manager, then owner. We got married, had kids, got kids through college, saved money, and retired. We first rented an apartment, then bought a house, and then a summer home. Now what?

Any goal can be easily missed or blown off course if you do not feel there is enough value or importance *to you*. Maybe you had tried dieting and experienced years and years of failure. Dieting when you were younger was maybe important because you were trying to look extra lean for the wedding pictures or to attract someone you had a crush on. Dieting now on special health foods might be important because your doctor told you to avoid certain foods because of health reasons. The reason why we are setting our goals can make the goal extra motivating. Past failures in attempting our goals can be tremendously discouraging and can make it easy not to try again. You will learn how to deal with these goal shortcomings. But we need to be ALL IN, where many times we're afraid to be ALL IN.

Imagine you are having lunch with an old friend who you have not seen in a few years:

- *You notice your friend is tremendously happy.*
- *They have a new hairstyle and new clothes.*
- *They are in good shape and have lost weight.*

You can't wait to find out why your friend is so happy. Is it a new hobby, new relationship, or maybe they won the lottery? Then they start telling you what is new. They started a new business, have a new challenge, or maybe a new relationship. Whatever it is, you can plainly see that they are challenging themselves, living a good life, living their life. As you sit back and listen to them what goes on in the back of your mind?

What do you think about?

- Are you jealous?
- Are you thinking that you don't have time to do the same thing?
- Do you think that they are just lucky?

Really? What's the difference between you and your friend?

From Dreams to Achievement

I grew up studying all the old-time gurus: Dale Carnegie, Norman Vincent Peal, Stephen R Covey, Jim Rohn, Earl Nightingale, Tony Robbins, and many more. When I studied to develop my mind and worked on building the mental strength to enlist methods found in books like "The Power of Positive Thinking," I realized I needed more, so I changed and added one word to it —**The Power of Positive Action**. Positive thinking is a good start but the actual action you take from it is what gets you what you want!

In recent years I keep my ideas active and motivated by enjoying newer released books by Jay Shetty "*Think like a Monk*," "*The Four Agreements*" – by don Miguel Ruiz and "*Can't Hurt Me*" – by David Goggins - They are all inspiring to me.

Almost all professional athletes, business executives, and many just regular people have life coaches. Many coaches help their clients focus on particular projects or goals and keep them positive and away from thinking about giving up.

Think of Positive Mental Action (PMA) on a couple's vacation to Florida. You planned to visit the beach to enjoy the weather and relax. Instead of sunshine, a rainy day comes roaring in and suddenly it might end up being the world's worst vacation to Florida. Alternatively, it could be the best. Maybe instead of everyone at the beach, you get to go bowling, play card games, or connect with quality time. Maybe during your rainy day, you got a chance to reconnect on a deeper level in areas that needed to be discussed. Now those discussions cleared up some very painful areas that needed help. The choices you make on a day-to-day basis, rain or shine, are a part of maintaining a PMA.

If you set goals and were *certain* about the outcome, what would you do? Let's say you're absolutely, without a doubt, positive about the outcome. Would you conquer them one by one, confident and anxiety-free? Maybe there was a time in your life when this was the case.

When your parents were in charge of you, at around two years old, did they decide that they were going to give you 5 to 7 attempts to learn how to walk, and if that didn't work out, you'd spend the rest of your life crawling? No, they let you try, over and over until you finally walked.

No option for failure was ever considered. So, if giving up was not an option, was that alone enough motivation to walk? What else is missing?

Assessment. Time. Encouragement. Those were there too when you were learning to walk. Your parents knew you didn't have a medical condition that kept you from walking. They gave you all the time in the world to learn and complete the task. All along they are making joyously squeaky sounds of encourage so you'll try until you've exhausted yourself. What if every goal in life could be achieved the way you learned to walk?

Remove your Limiting Thoughts and Actions
- *Look to other people who have done it before.*
- *At the beginning Confidence can be "faked."*

WITH consistency over time,
YOU can accomplish just about
ANYTHING

I did my first triathlon in my thirties. I was standing on the shores of a local lake with hundreds of other athletes, looking at the calm waters at sunrise and taking it all in. There were many different demographics, age ranges from teenagers to retirees, males and females of all body shapes and sizes. There were high polished physical specimens and others I will describe as the common man and others who were just getting started. My feet were squishy on the wet sand of the beach, half the people around me had wetsuits and I only had my swimsuit.

A wetsuit in a triathlon is typically not worn to keep you warm but to keep you buoyant. It keeps your body up on top of the water where it's much easier to swim. So, I was intimidated because I did not have the "right equipment."

My mouth was dry, and I had butterflies in my stomach. My head was killing me from nerves. The horn went off for me to swim. Every two minutes came another wave of 50 swimmers released into the race. Flailing arms and kicking legs were everywhere and even though I had trained for over 12 months for this big event and had "finished" from panicking in under four minutes, I found myself holding on to the side of a kayak of one of the lifeguards. I swam to shore, embarrassed and full of mixed emotions. But I resolved to sign up and try this again. I learned more about myself from that failure to finish. I knew it would make it so much sweeter when I could finally hit my goal!

You Need a Plan B

What big goals have you worked on and found that life bumped you off track, leaving you unsuccessful, at least for a short period of time? What detours did you need to take before you got back on track?

Success is never a straight line. You work hard, hit a bump, then tweak your plan, but don't lose sight of your goal. If an experience doesn't kill you, it makes you stronger.

You used to worry about your kids' friends. Were they bad influences? Would they cause your kids to end up spending the college fund on rehab? Maybe, in fact, that's what happened. It seems that warning kids about bad influences of any kind are more like giving them a shopping catalog of destructive habits rather than sound advice.

Apply the same standard of concern to yourself. Are the people around you conducive to you achieving your goal, or are they a hindrance? Be careful of the advice of close friends who seem to be dissuading you from being your best and enjoying your retirement the most.

Ask yourself, what are your self-limiting beliefs and where did you get them?

These limiters are mental, not real. But since you believe them, they carry the weight of reality. You are what you believe so if you believe you can do something or can't do something, you are right either way.

Work at letting go of your self-limiting beliefs. You will be able to think more freely when you look to attempt BIG GOALS. These limiting beliefs will get smaller and may go away especially over time when you can prove to yourself that you can achieve some of these early challenges and will make future challenges easier.

Don't limit your goals. These self-limiting beliefs can include ideas so ingrained we believe they are as true as the sun on a bright shiny day. These could be beliefs that you are bad at math, or you're unorganized. Maybe you were cut from a sports team in high school and that got you to back off from putting yourself out there. Maybe your parents complained about you sleeping in as a teenager, so you've believed all your life that you're not a morning person, or as a kid you were shy, so now you're not an outgoing person and can't meet new people. Your reaction to all of these examples is totally understandable but I challenge you. As a mature retired person take a risk on yourself— if you don't you may be missing many invigorating experiences.

So How do I Accomplish Big Bucket List Goals?

Equation # 1

Current Ability Level + Huge Amounts of Action = Success? (NO! -Not Enough – the equation is not that easy!)

This formula is incomplete. Huge amounts of action will not make you successful. It's like the old-school saying, "practice makes perfect." That's just plain wrong. The way it really should go is, "perfect practice makes perfect," meaning practicing the wrong thing, the wrong way, over and over is not going to get you to your goal. What it might get you is some minor successes or an excuse to quit.

A positive attitude from your parent probably helped you learn to walk. But was that enough on its own? So, what's missing?

Equation #2 is the one most people don't try; therefore, they don't improve like they thought they would.

Equation #2

Is more likely to get you the results you are looking for:

Current Ability Level + Huge Amount of Action + Adjustments + Repetition = Ongoing Circle of Improvement.

How to Develop Power of Positive Action in Your Life

Step 1: It takes practice. Realize that any time you train for something, you don't just do it once and become an expert. You practice doing it enough until it becomes second nature.

Step 2: You must be clear! You must know your exact non-wavering desired outcome

Step 3: Visualize the results you want

Step 4: Self-talk and affirmations

Step 5: Use visual rehearsals

Step 6: Continue working on Equation # 2

Fifteen years after my first triathlon, I was continuing to set goals of improving my triathlon finishing time. I was also challenging myself to different types of races. This sounds like I may have been an Adventurer character at the time. One summer my goals for a new triathlon were:

- **Finish a 70.3 Ironman Event – 1.2 Mile Swim, 56-mile biking and 13.1-mile run**
- **Good Finish time - under 6:00:00**
- **Dream finish time- under 5:30:00**

As you can see from the stats on the finisher's results, I beat my dream finish time by 1 minute and 30 seconds. I was so happy I had tears in my eyes finishing the event! What was different about this one vs. my first triathlon, where I panicked in the water and ended the race hanging on to the lifeguard's kayak? What are my clues to success here? They are very easy to find: I had 15 years of experience and probably 80 triathlons under my belt. I had better equipment (as in a wet suit). I had been a member for years of a local triathlon club that gave me mental and training support. However, my main reason for such an improved time was I hired a triathlon coach that year to customize my training—to push me when needed and to make me take off days when I needed to rest. In short, I found support and education in several ways to assist me in reaching my goal.

Equation #3 is the most likely way to get you the results you are looking for:

Current Ability Level + Huge Amount of Action + Adjustments and planning with a Coach + Repetition = Ongoing Circle of Improvement.

Equation # 3 helps keep you on track for important goals that you are passionate about. Having a triathlon coach with a new customized training plan each week was all the difference for me. Getting extra help and training for your goals will potentially get you to a higher level in your Bucket List and allow you to enjoy it more. It is so easy for me to see the parallel of me hiring a triathlon coach and me working with my clients as a financial advisor. You may feel better working with someone who has investment planning experience that aligns with your personal retirement goals. My coach helped guide me to set my PR— Personal Record!

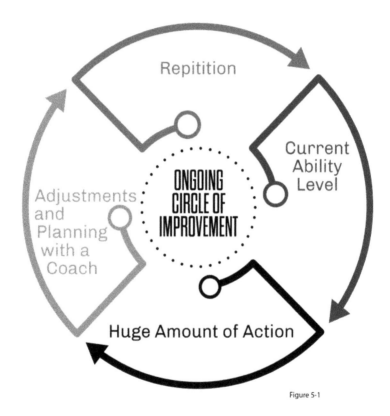

Figure 5-1

Try to put some balance setting goals in different focus areas of your life – this is easier said than done!

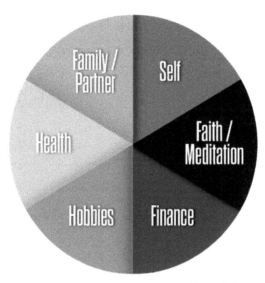

Figure 5-2

In the past, what goals did you attempt where you hit an obstacle and gave up? Maybe you moved to another project, in a different direction. Maybe it's a goal that is still not complete. Maybe it's time for you to look at it from another angle. Maybe you didn't give it enough time. You can accomplish your big goals with consistency over time!

So, when you look at your *new* or *old* Bucket List next time, you'll want to use the above formula to understand how important time and improvement are to accomplishing BIG GOALS. Success or failure is not a straight line. You adjust along the way. Some plan Bs are better for your happiness than the original plan A.

Ok now go for it and keep smiling!! Use the Big Bucket List Goal worksheet in the companion workbook to map out your path to success. You can complete this worksheet for each of your big goals and continue to adjust your approach as you go through the Ongoing Circle of Improvement.

Category (Self, Family, Faith, Health, Hobbies, Finance)	
What is the goal?	
Where am I now?	
How long will it take me to accomplish my goal?	
How can I work this into my current schedule?	
What resources do I need? (Coaching, Classes, etc.)	
Completed? ✓	

Figure 5-3

Chapter Six

Now Single, Divorced, Widowed

Contemplate Being Single Again

We typically plan to go through life without potholes in the road, but in reality, we all know that is wishful thinking. Many people reading this book are in a relationship with a partner. Many of your relationships may have begun when both of you were in your 20s, others more recent. Either way, a partner is someone you have with you through life's unknowns. Depending on your partner, this may be an advantage or disadvantage.

Social security statistics are eye-opening:

- Widowed individuals of both sexes account for 1 in 4 of the total beneficiary population aged 65 or older.
- Women account for more than half (56 percent) of the total beneficiary population aged 65 or older,
- Women account for the vast majority (78 percent) of widowed beneficiaries.

This chapter is for the unplanned single person. How does that happen? Typically, through death or divorce. If you are single now, I hope the earlier chapters may have already opened ideas for you. Perhaps you already have a routine that works for you. But no matter what evolves in life, you can always find ways to reinvent yourself to have your retirement the happiest it can be!

But for people on the doorstep of or in retirement, suddenly being single is a significant change.

This group of people is not small. Sadly, loved ones pass. You know it will happen, but many times, it happens early in retirement when you are relatively young, and you still have all your dreams and goals, many of them wrapped up in plans with your departed.

Also, you can be recently divorced and find yourself taking on new challenges you did not plan on handling alone.

What I'm going to do now is give a pep talk taken from ideas from previous chapters but tweaked for the single person:

Realistic Expectations

First, from Chapter 1, the newly single person must reassess their realistic expectations. You do not have to make all your changes from having a partner to being single overnight—give yourself a break and realize this will take time. The answers won't come in a single day.

Relationship professionals recommend not making any changes for at least 6 to 12 months to give yourself a chance to adjust. I would add especially do not make any *big* changes to anything quasi-permanent such as moving to a new state. On the other hand, you could try a fresh start in a new area in a way where you're not making a full commitment, perhaps by renting a house in your desired location to give it a try. The point is that there's no reason to make any immediate permanent changes other than maybe the desire to distract yourself with activity.

But burying yourself in making changes for change's sake doesn't free you from living with those changes. Once the distraction is over, what then?

Enjoy Your Memories

Enjoy the memories of the good times and always cherish them, but realize you are still on this earth and have a chance to impact yourself and your friends, family, and others in the community.

Know Yourself, Again

In Chapter 2, I asked you to look at how you felt you were supposed to be. Now you have the freedom to see yourself with fresh eyes and focus on the person who was always there but was perhaps muted to compliment your partner's traits and desires. So, go ahead and wake up that side up. You may love it!

You may see friends or family after your rediscovery and say, "I never wanted to do this hobby or adventure" or, that you are more passionate about charity work, or whatever your new or rediscovered passion may be.

Connecting with People

Take a look now that you are single and evaluate how "Chapter 3 – Connecting with People" applies to you? The three categories of connections that are the MAJOR Keys to Happiness still apply to you—maybe even more. Try to force yourself to reach out when you are ready. The Bucket List is for you. What's on your BUCKET LIST of desires? You have to ask yourself, "What is it that I want to try, learn, or experience?"

The idea of arranging your goals and getting the preparations done applies to you, and it's now more important than ever to see them through! Those Bucket List goals will become a social experience that is your lifeline to the world and a sense of fulfillment.

Once you're single, you will have a group of friends adjusting to you being single. You feel you are making all the adjustments, but your friends are also trying to figure things out. When you're newly divorced, they wonder if it's Ok to invite you, your ex, or both to an event. Do they invite you as an 'AND ONE' to dinners? When you are newly widowed, friends and acquaintances and family are also trying to process the changes and adjust.

It's up to you to let people know your thoughts.

There are only so many friends to go around. You don't want to lose any if you don't need to. Once you are ready, you can call partnered friends and ask if both of them—as a couple—would like to go out with you as the AND ONE. If you push through to this level, you will make it easier on yourself, your friends, and your family. It would be best to initiate the conversations with family to let them know you are Okay with being invited as the AND ONE. You need to let people know HOW to include you.

Don't Rule Out New Friendships with People of the Opposite Sex

There are many single retirees just like you, looking for companionship but uncomfortable about making the move. If you know someone who shares similar interests to you, don't be afraid to ask them out for a coffee.

Dating sites are popular ways to make new friends. You can find companionship on every level, including pressure-free relationships. And, who knows? One of your friendships could grow into a romantic liaison.

Platonic friendships can be rewarding and exciting without carrying the pressures of having to decide where this is going.

Finding new friends after retirement can be a challenge. You must know what you're looking for and overcome any apprehensions about being the first to reach out. It seems almost silly to worry about contacting people who share the same interests as you.

You deserve to have friendship in your life, and I hope you find people who make you truly happy!

Also, if you are reading this and you are not single, do not ignore your single, widowed, or divorced friends. Invite them to group parties, and make sure you try to meet for lunch or social events. Understanding the lives of your single friends during retirement can help give you a perspective that will help you frame the possibility of a life absent of a partner.

Epilogue
Putting It All Together

When I was writing this book, I thought I was going to need a last chapter that would bring all the chapters together. You know the grand finale!

Something to bring clarity, a wonderful conclusion, something very profound.

Let me ask what is a good way for me to wrap up the previous six chapters that you have read?

I have come to the conclusion that I have given you the tools you need to use and to work on.

It's now all up to YOU!

The previous six chapters are a road map. Read the entire book, do all the homework by yourself and with your partner, talk about things from your readings and the companion workbook. Make sure you and your partner listen and learn — use the book and the suggestions in it to help plan your retirement. Revisit the workbook exercises as you find yourself traveling through the retirement stages.

I hope you put some serious time into doing the exercises by yourself and with your partner. I think if you do, you will find it's fun and you'll discover a few key nuggets that you can work on and help to make your retirement years the best ones yet!

So now you don't have to ask—

What do you want to do for the next 30 years?

You know what you want to do!
Now go out there and live it and love it!

Please stay connected, give feedback and receive updates. Download the Free Companion workbook at **www.TedBuckley.com**.

Lightning Source UK Ltd.
Milton Keynes UK
UKHW021507080222
398332UK00001B/9/J